DON'T JUST BRAND THERE, DO SOMETHING

A BLUEPRINT FOR FINANCIAL BRANDS
THAT STAND UP, STAND OUT,
AND STAND THE TEST OF TIME

To Allison with warmest wishes and admiration.

WRITTEN AND ILLUSTRATED BY
MARTHA BARTLETT PILAND, CFMP

Don't Just Brand There, Do Something: A Blueprint for Financial Brands that Stand Up, Stand Out, and Stand the Test of Time

Copyright ©2025 Martha Bartlett Piland

All rights reserved. No part of this book may be reproduced or transmitted in any form or by any means, electronic or mechanical, including photocopying, recording, or by any information storage and retrieval system, without permission in writing from the copyright owner.

Published by Clovercroft Publishing
ClovercroftPublishing.com

Cover Design and Illustrations by Martha Bartlett Piland

Interior Design by Suzanne Lawing

Printed in the United States of America

ISBN: 978-1-956370-80-5 (print)

With deep gratitude:

To Gary Piland, who once said—and continues to say—"Why don't you? There's no reason you can't do that."

To my colleague Alexandra Reilly, CFMP for her brilliance, brains, and unwavering friendship.

To the many wonderful people in the financial industry I'm privileged to call clients, partners, and friends.

CONTENTS

Introduction	Don't just read this book. Do something.	11
Chapter 1	Create a Brand With Real Honest-to-Goodness Substance	15
Chapter 2	Seven Rules from This Book to Use Daily	17
Chapter 3	Brand ROI Is Hard to Measure. Do It Anyway	19
Chapter 4	5 Key Attributes of Every Successful Brand	25
Chapter 5	Common Branding Mistakes and What to Do Instead	31
Chapter 6	Four Models for Shaping Financial Brands	39
Chapter 7	Different Types of Branding Slogans and What They Can Do	57
Chapter 8	How to Find Your Actionable Big Brand Idea	77
Chapter 9	Setting the Stage for Productive, WOW-Filled Brainstorming Events	103
Chapter 10	Putting Your Brand into Action	133
Chapter 11	Pitfalls to Watch Out For	147
Afterword	Let's Go!	151

Introduction

DON'T JUST READ THIS BOOK. DO SOMETHING.

There are thousands—maybe millions—of buzzy books, podcasts, blogs, and videos about building financial brands. They trumpet tactics like paying trendy influencers or recruiting brand ambassadors.

They tell us to come up with that catchy slogan or super-edgy brand promise that guarantees your bank or credit union will stand out in this increasingly crowded marketplace.

But this is a marketplace where most financial institutions are viewed as commodities that simply hold and transfer money—like any other utility such as electricity or internet service that citizens and businesses need.

Where services are purchased on price and rate instead of value delivered.

Here's the problem.

Historically, services and products have been positioned that way. Low loan rates, high(ish) savings rates, and free checking are what have been promoted.

There's zero long-term profit potential in that position.

But we put lipstick on this pig.

So while we keep talking about great rates and freebies—and perhaps a toaster—in marketing promotions and sales calls, we tack on a slogan like "Your hometown bank,"

> For crying out loud, yes, please be bold. Or be loud. Or be something. But actually be it.

which doesn't differentiate your bank from the other community banks in the market, or "Be bold," which sounds interesting but there's no actual payoff.

It's time to do something.

I want you to build a brand with backbone. I want you to have a brand that actually brings something remarkable and valuable to employees and customers. A brand that people can see in action. A brand that makes you singular, special, and sticky.

This is the book that will help you do it. Let's go!

I hope you won't just jump to the TO DOs, but start with strategy and a solid foundation. OK, if you're curious, please look at the TO DOs. But don't start there. This is not a sprint. It's a marathon. So plan to do the exercises. Nobody likes burpees, but they make us strong. If you really want to win, you'll do the work and bring home the gold.

This book has theory, but the main goal is to leave you with inspiration to DO SOMETHING.

**Each time you see this icon *,
there's a challenge or an action step.**

**Each time you see a ! icon,
there's a brainstorm exercise to help you.**

Chapter 1

CREATE A BRAND WITH REAL HONEST-TO-GOODNESS SUBSTANCE

Your bank or credit union may already have some brand treasure buried deep in your DNA. It's your job to unearth it, polish it up, test it, and figure out how to execute it across every touchpoint for customers, employees, and suppliers.

Or maybe (gasp!) it's not there already and you have to create something from scratch.

This book is for three kinds of branders:

1) those who have no distinct brand position

2) those who have something to work with and haven't uncovered it yet

3) those who have a brand that's pretty good but could be awesome if they activated it

Whether you're branding a de novo bank or a well-established institution, building a brand with substance beyond the quippy slogan requires two things: 1) find something unique and ownable, and 2) take action with it. That means baking in actions that support this position throughout the entire institution.

If you can do that, no one—I mean no one—can stack up to you. That's because you have seized a position that delivers uniquely special value to customers and employees.

In the words of the great '80s philosopher MC Hammer, "U can't touch this."

Chapter 2

SEVEN RULES FROM THIS BOOK TO USE DAILY

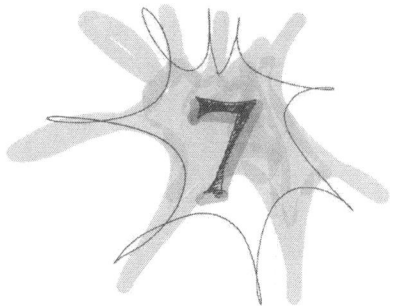

There are lots of DOs in this book. And seven things you should always remember. Why seven? Some call it the number of perfection. Nothing's wrong with that.

And while they're specifically related to being a DO-SOMETHING brand, they're pretty much good rules of thumb to follow no matter what.

1. You cannot be all things to all people. Stop trying.

2. Start where you can start. If you feel stuck trying to start at the beginning, start with an element you know

you can tackle. Then go back and work on the other pieces.

3. Research matters. Don't just rely on your gut. It might steer you wrong.

4. There's no such thing as perfect. Launch with a minimum viable product and keep improving.

5. Marketing is not an island. You cannot do this alone, so engage colleagues and outside resources or you will flare out.

6. Enduring brands, like Rome, were not built in a day. To do something magnificent, you must put in the time.

7. There will always be haters. There's not much you can do about them. So ignore them and don't let them tarnish your glow.

Chapter 3

BRAND ROI IS HARD TO MEASURE

How will you rationalize the expense? Developing or evolving a brand is expensive. It's a significant investment of time and money. So you have to do it for the right reasons, do it properly, and maximize its impact. And you must measure throughout the life of the brand.

You have to commit for the long term because a well-designed brand should last a long time.

Nike introduced its iconic *"Just Do It"* in 1988. The slogan and their signature swoosh logo have been the same for decades.

Invest wisely.

ALWAYS START WITH MEASURABLE GOALS

Measuring after the fact (after the act?) is difficult because it means backtracking, trying to find old benchmarks and making some things up.

Instead, begin with some clear goals for what you want to achieve. Do the hard work of figuring these things out before you launch into the fun creative part of the work.

Here are key areas you can measure and document to assess the success of your rebrand:

Audience Perception and Awareness

- **Brand Awareness:** Track how many people recognize your brand before and after the rebrand.

- **Brand Recall:** Measure how easily people can recall your brand when prompted with relevant cues.

- **Brand Image:** Assess how your target audience perceives your brand's personality, values, and positioning.

- **Brand Love:** Measure the emotional connection customers have with your brand.

- **Brand Loyalty:** Evaluate the likelihood of customers choosing your brand over competitors.

- **Brand Advocacy and Referral Rates:** Measure changes in the rate and quality of customer referrals.

Employer Brand and Culture

- **Employee Morale:** Measure employee morale and engagement with the new brand.

- **Turnover Rates:** Track employee turnover to assess the impact of the rebrand on retention.

- **Brand Advocacy:** Evaluate employees' willingness to promote the bank and its values.

- **Internal Brand Adoption:** Evaluate how well the new brand is integrated into internal communications, activities, events, and materials.

- **Board and Advisory Board Engagement:** Evaluate board members' willingness to refer and recommend your institution.

Financial Outcomes

- **Sales:** Analyze changes in sales revenue and growth rates.
- **Financials:** Compare your bank's performance to industry averages and competitors.
- **Market Share:** Track your market position relative to competitors.
- **Customer Acquisition Cost:** Measure the cost of acquiring new customers.
- **Customer Lifetime Value:** Assess the long-term value of customers.
- **Cost Savings:** Calculate the cost savings achieved through the rebrand (e.g., efficiencies that reduce marketing expenses).

> At Impressia Ban state a measurable desired impact right on their website: "Connecting women in business with more than bank products. We measure our impact by the improved financial health of women, their businesses and their families."

Online Metrics

- **Social Media Engagement:** Track likes, shares, comments, followers, and community growth. Evaluate the tone and emotions of people engaging with the brand.

- **Search Engine Rankings and Web Traffic:** Analyze keyword rankings and organic search traffic.

- **Lead Generation:** Measure changes in inbound loan and deposit inquiries.

- **Conversion Rates:** Measure website visitor conversions such as sign-ups, content downloads, forms filled out, or inquiries received.

- **Branch Traffic and Usage:** Monitor changes in the foot traffic to physical branches and usage of in-branch services, special events, and offerings.

> Climate First Bank reports measurable impacts including its positive environmental impact, solar lending platform, diversity, B Corp certification, impactful lending and financial growth.
>
> (2023 Impact Report www.climatefirstbank.com/our-impact)

Other External Considerations

- **Media Coverage:** Monitor the frequency, volume, and quality of media coverage about the new brand.

- **Community Engagement and CRA Impact:** Measure the impact of community engagement and corporate social responsibility initiatives. Track participation rates and public response to these activities.

- **Competitor Analysis:** Track competitor actions and responses to your rebrand.

Establish baselines on the things you want to measure for progress. This provides a "before and after" that makes the reporting you do later smart and compelling.

Chapter 4

5 KEY ATTRIBUTES OF EVERY SUCCESSFUL BRAND

Before we dig into how to do something that makes your brand really valuable, let's have a quick overview of why this is so important. Marketing and branding friends, you already know this. But in case you need support with others in the institution, use this handy reference.

A brand that brings long-term ROI generates 5 key attributes from its fans:

- People **TRUST** the brand.
- People **TALK ABOUT** the brand.
- People want to be **ASSOCIATED WITH** the brand.
- People **PAY MORE** for the brand.
- People are **LOYAL** to the brand.

Let's talk about trust.

People should have trust in their financial institutions. But in recent years headlines about bank failures, embezzlements, crypto schemes, and employees setting up false accounts in customers' names give us pause. Some bad actors and leaders who tolerate—or perpetuate—diseased corporate cultures have cast doubt on many others in the industry.

So you must work harder than ever to build and safeguard the trust of customers. Equally important is building trust with employees who interact with vendors and customers.

We're talking about you.

People who have a great—or a disappointing—brand experience have the chance to tell everyone they know, and thousands of strangers too.

It only takes a quick online search to find a huge outpouring of impassioned comments on social media, employment websites, and Google place pages. Listen to conversations at the local chamber of commerce mixer, the church social, the high school basketball game, or in line at the grocery store and you'll hear more.

Whether they're customers or employees, people are either evangelizing or warning others about their brand relationships.

Listen. Audit your own communications, but also Google your brand to see what pops up. Monitor social media and online review sites so you know what's out there. Don't stop with the consumer-facing reviews. Look at employment sites like Indeed and Glass Door to see what current and past employees have to say.

Jeff Bezos has famously said that your brand is what others say about you when you're not in the room. What are you giving people to talk about?

> Oooh - they're the ones who....

Where are the associations?

People demonstrate that they want to be associated with certain brands by:

- Wearing apparel with the brand's logo.
- Getting tattoos with the brand's logo.
- Carrying a handbag, insulated drink cup du jour, or other item with the logo.

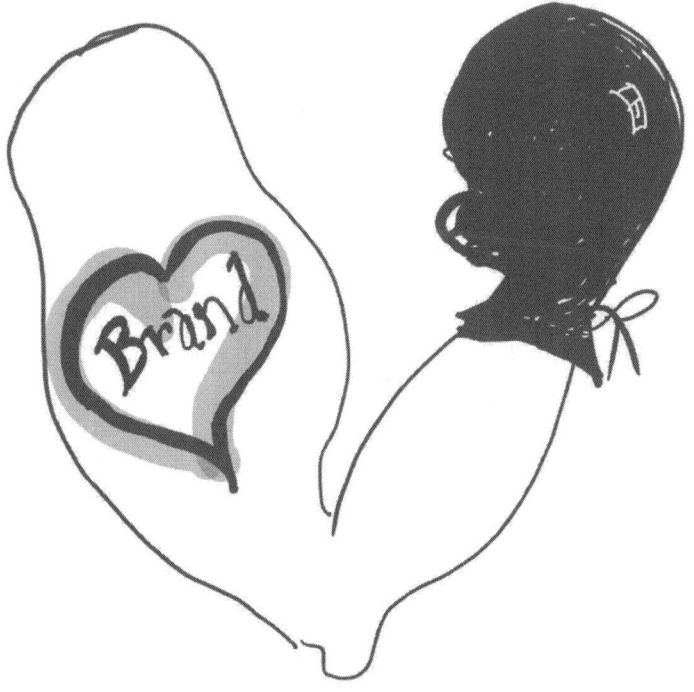

They also demonstrate their association with brands by the vehicle they drive, the phone they choose, the people they hang out with, and the cocktail they order. (Hendrick's, please.)

Look around: *You'll see brand associations everywhere if you take a moment to notice. Are customers and employees proud to be associated with your bank or credit union? What kinds of swag do they have with your name on it? Make sure it's high quality and accurately represents who you are and what you're about.*

What paying more really means.

Paying more for a brand we prefer could be the actual monetary cost, such as that rate that's not quite as competitive or the checking account with fees. But it could also mean:

- Time—driving farther to get to a branch.
- Hassle—being willing to put up with an inconvenience.
- Paying to acquire a logo'd item.

Conduct an online image search of "most popular brand tattoos" and you'll be surprised by what you see. That kind of brand affinity is stunning.

Ask questions: How do you quantify the "paying more" factor for your FI? Are you brave enough to raise some prices? Don't do it unless your brand promise and the value you deliver in exchange for that price is rock solid.

Are you asking employees to "pay more" by expecting them to volunteer for new projects in the institution, work late on occasion, or be visible in the community? Are they "paying more" by working on outdated equipment or not having all the tools available to do their best work?

Being loyal: enough said.

When customers return again and again, they bring revenue and profit if the bank's business is running correctly.

When employees stay longer than the average, that loyalty is ultra-valuable. Not only are they a wealth of institutional knowledge and experience, but the bank saves tremendously on the costs of hiring, onboarding, and training.

Think: *Do you know how many of your customers are loyal? How long are those relationships? What are they worth to your FI? How do they know if you appreciate their loyalty? Find out. Examine your average employee tenure to learn if attention is needed there as well.*

Chapter 5

COMMON BRANDING MISTAKES AND WHAT TO DO INSTEAD

Trying to please everyone. It can be oh-so-tempting to broaden the language of your promise—or to water it down—in order to jam in as many attributes as possible. In attempting to say everything, you say nothing at all.

It becomes like a dragnet used to herd fish into a corner, after which the fish are removed from the water with catch nets. Desirable fish are caught, sure. But this wide-sweeping effort also brought in fish they weren't seeking. Fish that weren't a good fit: fussy fish, fish that only want free checking, or fish that will flee to a better CD rate next month.

That position doesn't make anyone happy. Don't attempt it.

Instead, you need to be bold. Draw a line in the sand. Stand for something. Don't be afraid to stop chasing some

audiences. Let commodity-style "rate shopper only" prospects go.

You will never have enough people, money, or other resources to be all things to everyone.

Leading with "great customer service." Great service is a customer expectation, not a brand differentiator. You are supposed to have great service.

In fact, there are no brands that can get away with bad customer service for very long.

In the television show Seinfeld, the character of the Soup Nazi could abuse customers and even refuse to serve them if they displeased him. His "No soup for you!" epithet was accepted because his soup was so good that people were willing to put up with his abuse. It actually became a badge of honor. Sort of.

The Soup Nazi character was based on a real person and his successful (for a while) restaurant.

Your "soup" probably isn't that good. So if customers can't get good service, they can simply move on. Or lazily stay with you and feel stuck. However, they're the ones who gripe about your institution to everyone who will listen. Either way, the brand gets damaged.

> Don't you dare lead with "great service."

Flip side: If you're really going to base your brand on service, it should be astronomically, outrageously good. So good people can't stop talking about it. Better than the legendary service standards of Nordstorm, where stories are told about an employee who accepted a return of automobile tires. Nordstrom doesn't sell tires. Most financial institutions won't—and can't—go that far.

It's essential to take the time to decide and understand who you can serve really well, then excel at that. Do something. If you design and offer products, counsel, delivery systems and—yes, I said it, service—that they need and appreciate, you will be meaningfully different.

Saying something that doesn't really differentiate. Some banks are guilty of using a benefit or attribute as a substitute for their brand promise. Benefits are extremely important. But they rarely differentiate one institution from another unless they are intrinsically highly unique.

Many community banks are saying they're "the hometown bank" as if they're the only ones who are local. While it's fine to note that you're a local bank, that is not your brand. Too many others can claim that same position.

Many credit unions and mutual banks hang their brand on being "nonprofit and returning profits to our customers/members." That corporate structure may be a benefit, but it's not a unique brand position because every other competing credit union and mutual bank can say the same thing. Stop that.

A D&B search of banks in the United States yielded 1,138 institutions with "Farmers," 836 institutions with "Peoples," and 8,459 institutions with "First" in their names.

Trying to hobble along with a ubiquitous name. While a unique promise and customer experience are huge differentiators, a Generic National Bank name is an enormous hurdle to overcome. Since competition is not just across the street and around the corner—but across the country and beyond—a name that's easily confused with another spells trouble for your institution and its customers and prospects.

Some institutions attempt to solve this by shortening their name to a series of initials. NWBKS, CNB, and the like. That approach rarely solves the problem. It can be successfully done (like PNC) but from a consumer education and cost standpoint, it's a significant investment.

Evolving a load of initials that stand for a longer name into a human-sounding name or another word may be a strategic way to solve the acronym or initial dilemma and make the brand feel more accessible. For example, Fannie Mae is the Federal National Mortgage Association (FNMA) and Freddie Mac is the Federal Home Loan Mortgage Corporation (FHLMC). Fannie and Freddie sound like nice people.

According to its website, in 2005, Charles Schwab (schwab.com) launched a campaign, "Talk to Chuck," along with a suite of products designed to simplify retirement planning. Though this wasn't a name change, it was a way to tie back to the Charles Schwab name and make the brand feel more casual and inviting to regular people.

> You may not have the ability to rename your financial institution. If you don't rename, there's a vast amount of work needed to help differentiate your brand. If you do rename, there's a vast amount of work to be done to create awareness. Either way, there will be work.

It's human nature to shorten phrases, ideas, and names that are long. We like nicknames. We abbreviate things. Be aware of this if you're exploring renaming your bank. Don't just work on ideas for new names. Consider what your current or desired name might be shortened or evolved into. What are the merits of doing that?

In fact, many people have already shortened your name when they're referring to you. That new name may have already happened.

Saving money (being lazy?) and looking like everyone else. Investing in custom photography or illustrations can be expensive, so many financial marketers save money by using stock images or AI-generated images. There's nothing inherently wrong with that. But competitors are going to those same stock photo and AI wells for images, so it's likely that the photos you've chosen are going to be seen in other brands' communications—including non-financial brands.

That means using these tools properly requires curation and a disciplined process. Image choices must be part of a collective conceptual theme that hangs together as a whole and intentionally supports the brand personality. They're not just selected because they're cute or cool. They're selected for a reason.

Most ideal is an investment in custom photography to further differentiate your brand. If that's not feasible, use existing images strategically.

To make images more your own, you could:
- *Colorize them in a certain unique way.*
- *Crop them to highlight a specific visual element that tells your brand story.*
- *Add an overlay, a border, or other graphic treatment unique to your institution.*

We once created a rebrand package for one financial client who focused on areas of health and government programs. Their budget did not allow for custom photography, so we worked within parameters of stock photos. To avoid looking like others, we devised a visual system where all images would:

- Incorporate a circle.
- Use an image with associations to money, health, or government.

This approach resulted in a unified systematic approach to image selection. It supported their brand with an affordable and unique visual strategy. It was also flexible, so as more images were needed in the future, the client had a process to source additional photos that assured brand consistency.

Some banks use stock images with an overlay of a logo element to help these images feel more branded and create a consistent look across all media.

For example, Tucoemas Credit Union (tucoemas.org) uses an orange burst overlaid on photos to give emphasis and hearken back to its logo graphic. And photos are often presented in a circle, which coordinates with the circle in the center of the logo.

> **Don't look like everyone else.**

They also use some of these elements as type warmers. This pulls everything together nicely.

Successful branders have a process to ensure they manage every single brand touchpoint: lobby and drive-up graphics, online banking and mobile apps, collateral materials, social media, company swag, the sponsorship banner at the little league games, and the internal communications that go to employees.

Heartland Bank and Trust Company (hbtbank.com) takes a similar approach on its social media, but does not on its website. Ideally, this would be seen everywhere.

Chapter 6

FOUR MODELS FOR SHAPING FINANCIAL BRANDS

Typically, there are four different constructs for shaping financial institution brands. The problem is, one is really bad and it's the most often used approach.

1. BRANDING BASED ON PRODUCTS AND SERVICES

The brands that hang their hats on products are usually seen promoting High-Yield Savings Accounts, rebates, and checking with rewards. (And do regular people even know what the term Treasury Management actually means?)

They may still be promoting the number of branch locations or ATMs, or the fact that they have an online banking app.

Pros and Cons of Branding Based on Products and Services

There are no pros.

However, there are three cons:

For Marketing and the Bank

The need to spend more marketing dollars to elevate the brand's presence in the marketplace. Saturating the marketplace gets the bank into the top of the marketing funnel. But it's also expensive. The combination of high marketing expense and low margins means poor ROI.

This model makes it very difficult for the bank to make a profit.

Rather than promoting solutions they can bring, they talk about the means to those solutions. They're talking about light bulbs instead of an inviting, beautifully lit room. Don't sell light bulbs.

For Customers

Customers can get light bulbs anywhere at almost any price. There's no reason to be loyal. This is a race to the bottom.

For Employees

This example of branding does nothing to attract and retain excellent—or even good—talent.

I don't want you to pick this position. So please, look at the next three.

2. BRANDING BASED ON CUSTOMER EXPERIENCE

Customer Experience, or CX, is touted everywhere. When built properly, it has an incredible WOW! effect that makes people talk, stay, and evangelize on behalf of the brand.

Nordstrom, Publix Supermarkets, and Disney (who has its own Disney Institute to teach other companies what they've developed) have earned legendary customer experience reputations.

Note that there's a difference between customer service and customer experience. Customer service is being polite and answering a question or problem promptly and satisfactorily. Customer experience is about how the customers are made to feel throughout their entire journey with your brand.

Ally Bank is one who says they focus on customer service. Ally Bank: "**As a customer-obsessed company** with passionate customer service and innovative financial solutions, we are relentlessly focused on 'Doing It Right' and being a trusted financial-services provider to our banking, auto and corporate customers."

BANKING UNUSUAL: A UNIQUE CUSTOMER EXPERIENCE BRAND

We worked with a bank in the early aughts undergoing a new strategic plan as its leadership responsibilities were being taken on by the next generation of the family-owned bank. They served customers with branches in a wide array of markets across three states: located in large metros as well as small communities and some tourist spots.

The incoming leadership envisioned a different kind of banker and a new way of service delivery.

After in-depth research, visiting every branch, and detailed planning and exploration, we developed the Banking UNusual brand. The brand prescribed in detail the "not banking-as-usual" experience customers should have and how bankers would deliver it.

> **Banking UNusual did something.**

The rebrand of this bank included a new vision for the in-branch design with a strong emphasis on comfort and hospitality. The aroma of fresh-baked cookies permeated the lobby. Monolithic teller counters were replaced with comfortable furniture and universal bankers.

Hours were expanded. Bankers cleaned car windows at the drive-through and made in-person calls to customers for paperwork.

Advertising, collateral and web communications were fun, cheeky, and very visually different. Sponsorships, ribbon cuttings, and events were also anything but run-of-the-mill.

This was highly successful because every brand touchpoint was envisioned, designed, and measured against the brand promise that banking would be fun, different, and the opposite of the boring, business-as-usual banking many in the community were accustomed to expect and not enjoy. It was focused on helping customers in a way they wanted with a lot of fun and surprise mixed in, not just an idea the bank thought was fun and cool.

A brand based on CX can be challenging to build and deliver upon consistently, especially across multiple locations and markets. But it can be achieved with the right systems, processes, measurements, and training in place.

Pros and Cons of Branding Based on Customer Experience

For Marketing and the Bank

Marketing will need to work hand-in-hand extensively with other departments and business lines in the bank including IT, HR, training, operations, and others to build the systems and processes that make everything work.

It will also take a continuous, focused effort to build KPIs and measurable goals into the marketing plan, then report on them to measure, demonstrate, and deliver value to the bank.

This style of branding often doesn't naturally suggest logical choices for where to be involved in the community with sponsorships and board service because it's quite broad in nature. It's also quite broad in audience definitions, making media choices more challenging, and potentially more expensive.

For Customers

They look forward to being wowed, seeing something special happen to them and their financial lives, and they can see positive outcomes. They are likely to have more relationships with the bank. If the CX is exceptional, they will tell others and bring new customers in because of their word-of-mouth recommendations—both online and in person.

For Employees

Employees must be trained to WOW customers. But they also must be the recipients of WOW experience themselves.

They will need extensive training programs, guidelines, guardrails, and practice to deliver on a WOW CX promise. This must be an ongoing effort or it will be a flash in the pan.

With equal emphasis on an employee CX experience, talent attraction and retention will change for the better. Employees who feel valued and WOWed by the bank can be incredible ambassadors for potential customers and for referring others to join the team.

3. BRANDING BASED ON SERVING A SEGMENT

Women, veterans, family-owned businesses, Black communities, millennial solopreneurs … there are many groups of people who have particular financial needs and backgrounds that a bank or credit union can serve.

And while we would never advocate excluding anyone from banking with your institution, you can absolutely craft a brand that appeals to a segment of people with unmet needs and serve them very well.

Here are a few that stand out by their efforts (and quotes from their websites).

Black Communities

OneUnited Bank oneunited.com

"OneUnited Bank is the nation's largest Black-owned bank, with 50 years of service and two decades of digital banking. OneUnited serves as a digital navigation system (GPS) for financial services to help Black America and its allies close the racial wealth gap."

Military Personnel and Families

Armed Forces Bank afbank.com

"Founded in 1907 as Army National Bank and headquartered in Fort Leavenworth, Kansas, Armed Forces Bank as it was later rebranded is proudly serving active-duty, veterans, retirees, DOD, civilians, and their families in all 50 states and around the world."

First Command Bank: firstcommand.com

"The personal financial coach of our Nation's military families.® We coach your military family in their pursuit of financial security. First Command's reputation has been built on shaping positive financial behaviors through face-to-face coaching with hundreds of thousands of military families just like yours."

Roger Bank roger.bank

Roger Bank is a division of Citizens Bank of Edmond and focuses on military personnel. "Improving the banking experience for military members is a core mission for the team at Citizens Bank of Edmond, as many of us have served. Working alongside servicemen and women as they build wealth is deeply rooted in who we are and what we stand for."

Underserved Communities

Self Help Credit Union self-help.org

"Our mission is creating and protecting ownership and economic opportunity for all, especially people of color, women, rural residents and low-wealth families and communities.

"Self-Help helps women create economic opportunities for themselves and their families. We support women who are building assets by opening their first savings accounts, starting their own businesses, or buying homes. Our approach to community development also includes youth and education. We lend to child-care providers who might have difficulty getting loans from other sources, and we finance facilities for public charter schools that serve students poorly served by existing options."

Small Business Owners

Numerous banks say they're offering a great solution to small business owners. And there are several fintechs. One is Found.

Found found.com All-in-one banking for the self-employed. It offers banking, bookkeeping, tax, and invoicing services. While Found is a fintech, not a bank, it should give some inspiration to branders who want to be innovative and deliver huge value to customers in the small business space.

"Found is designed specifically for small business owners. Every feature built is designed with them in mind. Whether you are a freelancer, single-member LLC, S-corp or established business, Found will work for you."

Women

First Women's Bank firstwomens.bank

"First Women's Bank is on a mission to grow the economy and elevate the role of women within it. Women-owned businesses are growing 2x faster than the national average, yet they receive just 16% of all conventional business loans. It's time for a bank that's Banking on YOU.

"First Women's Bank is the only women-founded, women-owned and women-led commercial bank in the country with a strategic focus on the women's economy. Our clients are entrepreneurs, innovators, and leaders—moms, daughters and caregivers. So are we."

Impressia Bank impressiabank.bank

"Impressia Bank is built for women in business, by women in business.

"The women's economy is growing at twice the rate of other businesses, yet Banks and Fintechs are not yet meeting the needs of the growing 'sheconomy.' We're here to change that. As a woman business owner, you have enough hurdles, let us help you remove some of them."

Other Verticals

Esquire Bank esquirebank.com

Esquire offers a full suite of products and services for businesses, but—as its name indicates—has a large focus on financial services for law firms. Law firms have very unique banking needs. Some require financing for long litigation processes like class-action suits and contingency cases. Others need working capital based on assets that don't show up on the balance sheet. Esquire, who also has lawyers on its team, works to bring special expertise and solutions to its lawyer customers.

> Wait. This is scary: We can't just abandon our customers and go down a new path.

Wait. This is scary: We can't just abandon our customers and go down a new path.

Marketers reading this book may say there's no way to build a new brand based on a customer segment. But what if you carved out a segment and designed a brand that's meaningful to its members?

I don't mean just say, "Community First People's Bank's small business division." I do mean do something that answers an unmet need in a very unique way.

For instance, Impressia Bank mentioned above is a division of CNB Financial Corporation.

In another example, Her Bank by Legends Bank is also a separately branded arm of a traditional full-service institution.

Her Bank by Legends Bank her-bank.com

"Her Bank is a brand inspired by women for women to create a perfect blend of personalized banking with a modern touch. We pair consultation and customization with technology and resources to provide a holistic approach to help you achieve your financial goals.

"Note: Her Bank is a brand of Legends Bank. Legends Bank is Member FDIC and Equal Housing Lender. All products and services are provided through Legends Bank. For more information, visit legendsbank.com."

Banc of California also took this approach to serve a specialized market with its SmartStreet brand.

Banc of California has a division of its business branded SmartStreet. It's dedicated to homeowners' associations because those have very specific, unique needs. Anyone who's been part of an HOA knows there are multiple issues with dues, maintenance fees, and other issues that require financial management by people who have day jobs.

"Customized automated banking solutions and simplified financial management for community management companies and their homeowner clients." bancofcal.com/specialty-banking/community-associations/

> Your brand should alleviate headaches.

There are a lot of headaches. SmartStreet is designed to address that pain.

Pros and Cons of Branding Based on Serving a Segment

For Marketing and the Bank

Marketing may face a big burden with data analysis among current customers as well as analysis of the geographic areas where branches are located to find more of the customers who they can best serve.

However, depending on the bank or credit union's structure, geography may not be a limitation at all, which further opens opportunities to serve specific audiences with special needs.

A different talent hiring strategy may be needed. For example, Esquire Bank has attorneys on its team. They helped develop the services the bank offers, but they also can "talk the talk" to their customers and prospects because they have walked in their shoes. That adds up to credibility, as well as financial products that uniquely serve the intended audience.

Marketers who adopt this style of branding can make decisions about where to be involved in the community with sponsorships and board service far more easily. Rather than sifting through requests for donations and volunteers from far and wide, choices can be narrowed to those that are aligned with the group they're serving. The same applies to sponsorships and media-buying choices.

For Customers

Current customers may feel left out—unless the new brand is positioned in such a way that they still feel valued and included.

Customers and prospective customers who fit into the segment will feel heard and valued if all the other brand delivery pieces are in place throughout the customer journey.

For Employees

Not all employees may feel a part of the segment, or feel excited to serve that segment. On the flip side, it does offer exciting opportunities to attract and retain those who do, and deepen those relationships with them as well as the customers.

Additional training may be needed. Even if every single employee is excited about a new direction or segment, it's likely that they won't all know the best ways to ask questions and understand the customer needs in order to recommend the right solutions. Consider whether employees may need to get some outside training or certifications to help them be successful in their roles.

4. BRANDING BASED ON PURPOSE

Purpose can be a powerful rallying point for people who hold some beliefs or issues in common. They can feel more connected and quite excited to bank with an institution that's in the center of those values.

That could mean doing business with a certified B Corp—or it could mean simply working with bankers whose visions align with theirs.

It can be a win-win-win relationship.

When people think about a brand based on purpose, environmental issues may be one of the first examples that come to mind. Climate First Bank and Walden Mutual Bank fit into that category. But there are other examples, too.

Climate First Bank climatefirstbank.com "The world's first FDIC-insured community bank dedicated to the environment and sustainability."

Walden Mutual Bank waldenmutual.com "We enable anyone to make positive and lasting change to our local food ecosystem."

There are others with a strong non-environmental purpose that should also be noted.

Amalgamated Bank amalgamatedbank.com/who-we-are "America's Socially Responsible Bank. Empowering organizations and individuals to advance positive social change.

"We're the bank for people who care what their money does in the world. When you deposit your money at Amalgamated, it supports sustainable organizations, progressive causes, and social justice. We are committed to environmental and social responsibility. We're net-zero and powered by 100% renewable energy, and we have a long, proud history of providing affordable access to the banking system, supporting immigrants and affordable housing, and being a champion of workers' rights."

Christian Community Credit Union mycccu.com

From its website, "Christian Community Credit Union (CCCU) is a faith-based, purpose-driven financial co-operative whose mission is to serve Christ followers to live and give more abundantly. For over 67 years, we've provided individuals and ministries with the financial tools and knowledge they need to grow and thrive financially, so they can transform our world through their generosity.

"The money you deposit in the Credit Union helps churches grow, ministries expand, and individuals thrive. Whether it's constructing or remodeling a new church building or funding a home loan, your money is working in the Christian community.

"At CCCU, giving is in our DNA. When you use our credit and debit cards for purchases, you're giving to Christian causes. To date, CCCU has donated more than $6 million to ministry and mission projects in the U.S. and around the globe. Simply put, your everyday purchases help change lives."

Note that CCCU also has a business unit that specifically serves churches and the specific financial needs pastors would have for buildings, payroll, treasury management, and other unique needs for managing the banking functions of the ministry.

> Having a defined purpose seems to be a challenge for many banks. There are many marketing slogans based on ubiquitous themes like "big enough to serve, small enough to care," "high tech, high touch," and "your bank for a lifetime."

Pros and Cons of Branding Based on Purpose

For Marketing and the Bank

The mission, vision, and values of the bank may be outdated and dusty, or may have lost their meaning. It's quite possible that nobody in the bank can articulate them. Marketing may have difficulty evolving or changing these, however, because they could be considered "sacred" inside the institution.

Marketing will need to work hand-in-hand extensively with the C-suite. Going as far as Climate First or Walden Mutual may be too far of a stretch for an established "we're for everyone" community bank.

As with serving a certain segment, marketing may still have that heavy lift with data analysis among current customers as well as analysis of the geographic areas where branches are located to find more of the customers whom they can best serve.

However, depending on the bank or credit union's structure, geography may not be a limitation they encounter, which further opens opportunities to serve audiences whose values align with a certain purpose or issue.

For Customers

Existing customers who share this purpose will be amazed and thrilled, as will prospective customers. But depending on how far a brander decides to go, some customers may also be alienated and feel like they're no longer important to the bank. They could move on.

Good communication with them through all levels of the evolution is extremely important.

> Millennials and Gen Z are especially interested in working for and buying from companies who share their values.

For Employees

The same can be said for talent attraction and retention. Some may embrace a shift in focus, while others won't.

Millennials and Gen Z are especially interested in working for and buying from companies who share their values. So if a goal is to attract more next-generation employees and leaders, an employer brand that's about making a difference will have a very strong pull with these people who represent the potential leadership and the future of the institution.

IT MAY BE SCARY, BUT YOU MUST DO SOMETHING.

Marketers reading this book may say there's no way to build a new brand based on anything other than what they already have.

I don't entirely agree. But if that's true, then understanding what that existing brand is now, and what it can be—when it's supported by actions—may be the way forward.

If so, this book is still for you. You can still DO SOMETHING. You must.

Don't Just Brand There, Do Something

COMPLIANCE, COMPLIANCE, COMPLIANCE

As you're exploring any kind of focused brand approach, whether it's based on audience, purpose, or experience, involve Compliance at the outset.

Involve Compliance at the beginning to be sure all the bases are covered.

You want to ensure that the position you take is selected and activated ethically and responsibly. Even with the best intentions, it's possible that you could unknowingly start down a path that puts your financial brand at risk.

The goal is to be inclusive and not take advantage of a group of people. Or even appear to have an intent in exclusion or harm. Always involve compliance.

Chapter 7

DIFFERENT TYPES OF BRANDING SLOGANS AND WHAT THEY CAN DO

Slogans can work in a variety of ways. As you're exploring what you want to convey in your promise, you can also think about *how* you want to convey that information.

There are different foundational structures or categories a tagline may fall into—sometimes more than one. The list below is a good reference with examples from widely known consumer brands as well as from financial brands. It will help you consider what type of approach will feel authentic for your institution.

No matter the direction you take, your goal is for the slogan to eventually become shorthand for your story: for customers and for employees.

Describe a Benefit

A slogan can quickly tell potential customers what the brand offers and how it will improve their lives. Walmart tells people they can "Save money, live better." The promise is that they'll get quality products that improve their lives for less money than they'd spend elsewhere.

In banking, the easy fallback is to talk about products instead of solutions. But every institution has similar products, so leading with them is a mistake.

Extolling benefits helps people envision connecting with the brand in a way that solves their needs. **Community First Credit Union** in Wisconsin promises *"We'll Find A Way!"* That tells prospective customers it has a can-do attitude that can help them get their financial need done.

"We'll Find A Way!" might also relay to employees that the credit union will help them find a way. That could be for growing their careers, balancing personal and work life, or helping them reach their financial dreams.

For many years, **Discover Card** has said, *"It pays to Discover."* While this tagline likely began with their groundbreaking 1.5% cash back rewards (and they now have more competitors in the rewards space), Discover still offers unique value to its customers through perks and benefits such as redeeming the rewards at any time and in any amount they choose.

> Some brands change their slogan every whipstitch. That's a waste of money and confusing to audiences. A slogan that effectively does something is designed to last much longer.

Speak Frankly

A Google search says the tagline *"We suck less"* has been ascribed to several companies. Most convincing to me is the attribution to a CAD company where its CEO proclaimed "we suck less" from the main stage at an international user convention. It's said that he straightforwardly admitted that all the products in the field were unwieldy and not user friendly... and that his was the least worst. That was bold. It can be a tricky proposition to use something like that as a starting point.

PNC Bank executed this frankness approach very well with its recently unveiled slogan *"Brilliantly Boring since 1865."* That slogan is a smart counter to grabby headlines about bank failures, embezzlements, and pig butchering schemes that made some consumers concerned about the health of their financial institutions.

PNC answers these concerns by touting a promise of being dependable, trustworthy, and un-flashy with customers' money so they can be confident their money will be there—allowing their lives to be fulfilling. "Which is pretty un-boring, when you think about it," PNC's website states.

PNC's creative approach has garnered significant earned-media exposure and online engagement because of its unusual angle.

PNC's choice is more attention-getting and memorable than a slogan like: *"Consistent, Strong & Dependable"* or others that are very straightforward and quite commonplace. They are saying something similar, but the *"Brilliantly Boring"* concept resonates with much more impact. It also leads to some very interesting ways to innovatively deliver on the promise.

It might take some imagination to envision how this promise could work for PNC's employer brand.

Abbey National Bank's *"Because life's complicated enough"* and **Allegacy FCU's** *"Unlike Your Bank"* also make frank promises that stand out and can be acted upon.

Ask a Question

A question can be a smart way to grab attention and get people thinking about the brand's message. *"Have you driven a Ford lately?"* challenged consumers to question and perhaps rethink their perceptions of the auto maker.

Capital One asks, "What's in your wallet?" to help consumers question if the cards and cash in their wallets are really serving them as well as Capital One promises it can.

For extra credit: if Capital One customers answer, "Capital One," in their minds when they hear the question, this is also beneficial. It serves to reinforce that they've already made a wise decision.

> Caution: Don't ask a question if you won't like the answer.

As in the PNC example, this tagline may not be as strong for internal marketing to employees and prospective talent.

Caution: Don't ask a question if you won't like the answer.

On The Financial Brand's article, "The World's Biggest List of Bank Slogans—Over 1,100 Financial Taglines" (thefinancialbrand.com/bank-slogans/) very few institutions listed are asking a question in their taglines.

Create a Sense of Identity

A slogan can help to define the brand's personality and values. That lets potential customers think about whether they share the same values and would be a good philosophical match. For example, Apple's *"Think different"* captures the innovative and creative spirit of the brand to attract people who see themselves in that same light.

Banks and credit unions can also do this successfully if they have a solid understanding of their customer base. A few from The Financial Brand's list that stand out:

- **California Federal Bank**—*"You have more power than you think."*
- **Scotiabank**—*"You're richer than you think."*
- **USAA**—*"We know what it means to serve."*

Each of these slogans projects a sense of WE: a certain kind of banker relating with a certain kind of customer with a shared sense of identity and beliefs about financial matters—and life. These slogans invite the listener to belong.

Evoke an Emotion

Other slogans may trigger positive feelings about a brand, such as happiness, trust, or nostalgia. Disneyland's *"The happiest place on earth"* fosters an emotional connection with its audiences that begins with first the desire to visit, then the anticipation of visiting, the visit itself, and the afterglow. Disney designs and delivers an entire emotional journey of joy and wonder.

Money is highly emotional too. Financial institutions who can forge a positive emotion around their brands have the opportunity—and the challenge—of differentiating themselves in a very different way.

In other examples, **Fidelity Bank's** *"Bravely onward,"* and **NorStates Bank's** *"Think Possible"* offer internal and external audiences something inspiring, uplifting, and different to believe in.

Introduce a Brand Value

A slogan can be a powerful way to showcase the brand's core values. L'Oreal's longtime slogan, coined in the early '70s, *"Because you're worth it,"* urges consumers to place value on themselves, promising that they deserve a glamorous and maybe more expensive product.

Target's purpose statement is *"To help all families discover the joy of everyday life,"* and its mission statement is *"The promise of surprises, fun, ease and inspiration at every turn, no matter when, where or how you shop."* Their devoted shoppers often brag on finding fabulous items at "Tahhr-jeh," mimicking a French accent and rejoicing in their fancy finds at great prices.

Building a sense of community around the brand by appealing to a shared interest or values can go many different directions. **Citizens Bank's** *"Good Banking Is Good Citizenship"* highlights its values of community investment and civic responsibility while also appealing to people who admire and share those values. It feels patriotic and as American as scouting, baseball, and apple pie.

Ardent Credit Union's *"Grit makes great"* and **Zeal Credit Union's** *"Hard Working Americans Bank On Us!"* convey values of self-sufficiency, resourcefulness, and the dignity of work. These are also values that marry well with stewardship of money and satisfaction in a job well done and will appeal to a group of like-minded individuals.

Christian Community Credit Union's *"Serving Christ followers to live and give more abundantly"* highlights a belief in serving people with values of faith-filled living and tithing from their income. It's a straightforward way to demonstrate a fit for people who share their ideals.

Differentiate from Competitors

Some slogans are designed to help a brand to stand out from the crowd and position itself differently in the marketplace. *"The Brawny Paper Towel"* uses a memorable lumberjack character to differentiate itself from other paper towel brands. In this case, the name is repeated in the slogan and conveys a tough, hard-working, no-fuss and high-value paper towel.

> A caveat to a "local" positioning: while it separates a community bank from the larger out-of-town banks, it does not differentiate the institution from other locals who have also been around for a long time. It may also hinder the bank in future M&A activities.

The slogan from **Blackhawk Bank & Trust**, *"We're Not For Sale,"* has a dual meaning indicating that it has high integrity and also isn't open to being acquired by an out-of-town bank. They're local. **Frost Bank's** *"We're from here"* also says it's local, with the added inference that its bankers understand the local people and local economic landscape like outsiders won't.

Central Bank's *"We Don't No!"* is a clever way to position itself against other banks who are perceived as likely to quickly turn down a customer's loan application or be unwilling or unable to serve their other financial needs.

Be Catchy or Incorporate an Element of Fun

A slogan should be easy to remember and repeat, so that it stays with people long after they've seen or heard it. For example, *"I'm lovin' it"* from McDonald's is short, catchy, and easily remembered.

A touch of humor or playfulness can make a brand more human and relatable. Frito Lay's *"Betcha Can't Eat Just One"* uses this kind of lighthearted approach to highlight the addictive nature of their chips.

Some financial brands that fit this category:

- **GEICO**—*"So easy a caveman can do it."*
- **People's Bank**—*"Banking Unusual"*
- **WaMu**—*"Whoo hoo!"*

Caution: Being fun or catchy simply for the sake of entertainment isn't strategic. Though a witty tagline may have a strong appeal, it still must convey a benefit, differentiate from competitors, or serve as some sort of rallying cry. The examples above stand on their own without requiring additional explanation. Enough said.

Trying to be too cute can also wear thin. The online check deposit app of one major bank has a joke about unicorns and how users shouldn't endorse their check with a sparkly pen. That was charming the first few times. Two years and thousands of transactions later, it just seems dumb.

Play Off of the Name

Slogans that play off of the institution's name can help the whole brand package be more recognizable in a crowded field. It's also harder for a competitor to mimic.

Some examples of this approach include:

- **Intrust Bank**—*"I trust INTRUST."*
- **KeyPoint Credit Union**—*"Get more. That's the point."*

- **Members First Credit Union**—*"Our Name Says It All!"*
- **Metlife**—*"For the if in life."*

In the best examples, playing off of a name builds name repetition and familiarity because the name—or an evolution of it—is being spoken twice.

If the bank is entering a new market, this approach—especially if it's also fun and catchy—can be extremely valuable in helping boost brand awareness more quickly.

Inspire Action

Motivating people to take action, whether it's trying a product, visiting a store, or supporting a cause is a powerful tool in the marketers' hands. Nike's slogan *"Just Do It,"* which debuted in 1988, emphasizes the motivational and emotional aspect of their athletic wear. It's a no-excuses, empowering message of self-fulfillment. It inspires people to get up off the couch, the bench—or wherever they are—and move.

Some actionable, believable slogans from financial institutions:

Brookline Bank—*"Bank here. Get there."*

Union Bank of California—*"Invest in you."*

Ally Bank—*"Do It Right."*

BOS Bank—*"Get more BANK for your buck."*

These examples are active. They're positive and empowering. Interestingly, they put responsibility on the listener. And like Nike's slogan, they offer opportunity for self-fulfillment.

Promise an Experience

A slogan can hint at the kind of experience that customers can expect when they interact with the brand. Coca Cola's

"*Open Happiness*" suggests that their product brings not just refreshment but joy.

U.S. Bank promises "Five Star Service Guaranteed." They have extremely high customer service standards and monitor regularly via phone surveys and in-app messages to be sure that what's being delivered is what they promise.

What's unclear in this promise is what they'll do if a customer does not receive five-star service from the bank.

Some other experience promises:

Downey Savings—*"The Friendlier, Easier Place to Bank"*

First Entertainment Credit Union—*"An Alternative Way to Bank"*

First National Bank of Long Island—*"Where Everyone Knows Your Name"*

It's a very tall order to promise and deliver on a service or experience proposition. It does offer many exciting possibilities for branding and DO-SOMETHING marketing efforts. But if you choose this approach, be sure you have buy-in across all department and business lines in the institution. Even further, make sure they'll roll up their sleeves to pitch in and help. Their support and ownership are vital to ensure

> Note that there are hundreds of banks promising some kind of wonderful experience. Unless you can consistently deliver a Nordstrom-style experience, you should take a different route. Everyone says they have great service.

that all the mechanisms are in place to make your promise a reality.

Otherwise, you'll just have a pretty little (meaningless) slogan.

Appeal to a Specific Audience

A slogan can be crafted to directly appeal to the brand's ideal customer. For example, *"Maybe she's born with it, maybe it's Maybelline"* uses targeted language to connect with women who want to enhance their natural beauty. (Or to appear as if their beauty is effortless and natural.)

While banks and credit unions can never appeal to one audience at the expense of excluding another, building a brand around serving a certain audience can bring great value to the people in that group. As marketers, make sure that while you're letting people know who you can serve best, you welcome any customer who wants to do business with you.

Here are a few audience-specific banks that stand out:

- **Her Bank by Legends Bank**—*"A better banking experience for women."*

- **Bluevine**—*"Business banking that gets you more for your money."*

- **Grasshopper Bank** (for small businesses and start-ups)—*"Only forward."*

These banks can serve anyone, but they offer services and products designed to serve specific needs—often unmet needs—of a specific group of people.

Embrace a Cause

A slogan can underscore the brand's commitment to a social or environmental cause. For example, Toyota's *"Think green, drive green"* highlights the automobile's eco-friendly features.

Building a reputation around embracing a cause can be a powerful way to build a DO SOMETHING brand.

Causes can range from environmental, to faith-based, to social issues. They can also address health, education, and economic development. The choices are probably endless, because there are many growing needs that banks and credit unions can use their influence and funds to address.

> No "First National Community Citizens" here. The tagline and name together are strong pairings worth more than the sum of their parts.

Hope Credit Union (hopecu.org) "HOPE (Hope Enterprise Corporation, Hope Credit Union, and Hope Policy Institute) provides financial services, leverages resources, and engages in advocacy that strengthens the financial health and wealth of people in under-resourced Deep South communities." Their slogans: *"Brighter futures begin with Hope"* and *"Hope makes it happen."*

Here are some others to spark conversation with your team:

- **Christian Community Credit Union**—*"Your Money Building God's Kingdom"*

- **Climate First Bank**—*"Bank like tomorrow depends on it."*

In these examples, the slogans do most of the work to tell the story, but are supported by the institutions' names.

No "First National Community Citizens" here. The tagline and name together are strong pairings worth more than the sum of their parts.

This approach may be one of the easiest by which to make decisions about choosing sponsorships, community service, social media, and advertising channels. It also allows employees and customers to easily self-select your bank or credit union. They either share a desire to support this cause or they don't.

Some institutions are founded this way at the outset. Some transform into a cause-focused bank as part of their growth and evolution. And others (similar to the case of Her Bank by Legends Bank) may establish a cause-based offshoot while leaving their original brand intact.

> The employer brand must be part of this development equation, not an afterthought.

Chief Marketing Officers who take this blended brand plus sub-brand option will have two entities and two budgets to manage. Keep this in mind if you're considering going this route.

Include Employees

Employees are a vital audience. They can make or break the launch of a new brand or making an existing brand more powerful. Ideally, a slogan that's outward facing also works for your employer brand.

Your employer brand should be inseparably married to your outward-facing brand. Employees devote a significant portion of their lives to the bank. They've chosen this institution over other employment opportunities.

At times, they'll prioritize the institution's and customers' needs over their own self-interests. It means they may miss time with family, hobbies, or other passions in order to help fulfill your mission.

The bank owes them more than a paycheck. It owes them follow-through on a mission and brand promise that includes them.

So after you've muddled around on the examples from the previous pages, take a second look at them. Imagine how those slogans could be used as-is or adapted for internal audiences. Consider how they could be used to define actionable ways to help employees find professional development and fulfillment. That's one key element of talent attraction and retention that can't be overlooked.

Some banks whose strong employer brand stands out:

For employee leadership and development

Old National Bank: oldnational.com, headquartered in Evansville, Illinois, has launched several CEO Council cohorts with a diverse group of high-potential leaders from throughout the organization. The purpose of Old National's program is to accelerate their development as leaders, as well as to advise the CEO and executive leadership team on multiple topics that affect the bank, its customers, and team.

Regions Bank: regions.com, established a great employee development program with a distinct name and brand personality that fit with the bank's overall brand. And like a good consumer brand, it offers a promise and fulfills it. Regions Bank, headquartered in Birmingham, Alabama, created RegionsLEADS for its 20,000+ associates. The LEADS acronym supports the bank's core values and delivers on a promise to support the career development, engagement and well-being of associates as an employer of choice. "We love an acronym," says Shannon Knabb, leadership development program manager at Regions who headed up the program development. "It makes it easy to remember, but it also really connects with what our purpose is."

> "Everyone" isn't just external customers. It's Huntington colleagues too.

For employee pride and inclusion

Huntington Bank: huntington.com, in Columbus, Ohio, is quoted in the media as saying they believe "putting people first—our customers, colleagues, and communities—is at the very core of everything we do." Their vision is stated as becoming "the leading 'people-first, digitally powered' bank."

Those are big promises that may not be completely unique. But what does make Huntington National Bank unique is the way they work to live up to these promises for all customers: both internal and external.

They're not afraid to think outside the normal industry approach to customers and employees. They were featured in Banking Dive for one such example.

Huntington National Bank partnered with the Magnusmode app to help neurodiverse people bank better. Together, they've created free step-by-step guides on everyday tasks like depositing checks, withdrawing money, and disputing charges.

The bank's chief diversity, equity, inclusion, and culture officer said, "We believe that everyone deserves a shot at financial success."

"Everyone" isn't just external customers. It's Huntington colleagues too.

The step-by-step guides feature two Huntington colleagues who joined the bank through its Autism2Work program, which has provided workforce training and employment opportunities for neurodivergent adults, including those with an autism spectrum disorder. Employees gave input on the topics the guides cover.

Huntington Bank's app has cards to help neurodiverse customers bank more easily. They were designed with the help of neurodiverse colleagues.

Not only is Huntington making the bank and its services more accessible to neurodiverse customers, they also seek to invest in a diverse workforce that includes neurodiverse people. In other words, they work to address serving all internal customers.

Just a few of the things they offer:
- cultural celebration day
- week of cultural celebration

- colleague appreciation week
- annual diversity, equity, inclusion, and culture awards
- tuition reimbursement and tuition pre-imbursement programs
- dependent scholarships
- business resource groups
- inclusion councils
- communities of practice
- military benefits
- volunteer opportunities

Huntington says that many of the business decisions the bank makes includes input from colleagues. That ensures they continually work across all areas of the bank to keep the mission alive.

In later chapters of this book, we'll talk more about employees and the brand promise you must make to them.

Slogan DON'Ts

1. Caution: If you have non-English speaking audiences or people who don't have English as their first language, be careful about translations and cultural differences. You could make some blunders.

> Three. Word. Tagline. I have never been a proponent of taglines like this. They're not as memorable and they become quickly dated. "Simpler. Better. Faster." Just don't do this!

2. Please, no three-word taglines with periods between the words. They're. Already. Outdated.
3. Don't use clichés that can become outdated quickly or you'll come across as out of touch.
4. Don't be the unwitting copycat. Google your concepts. There's so much already out there, it's hard to be unique. But unique you must be.
5. Don't appropriate other brands. The famous "Got Milk?" campaign has been pirated thousands of times with "Got (fill in the blank)?" by other companies. It's cheap and lazy.
6. Don't be too long. Try to keep it to eight or fewer words so it's more easily remembered.
7. Don't use jargon that's only specific to the banking industry. That insider language puts up a wall in front of customers and prospects.

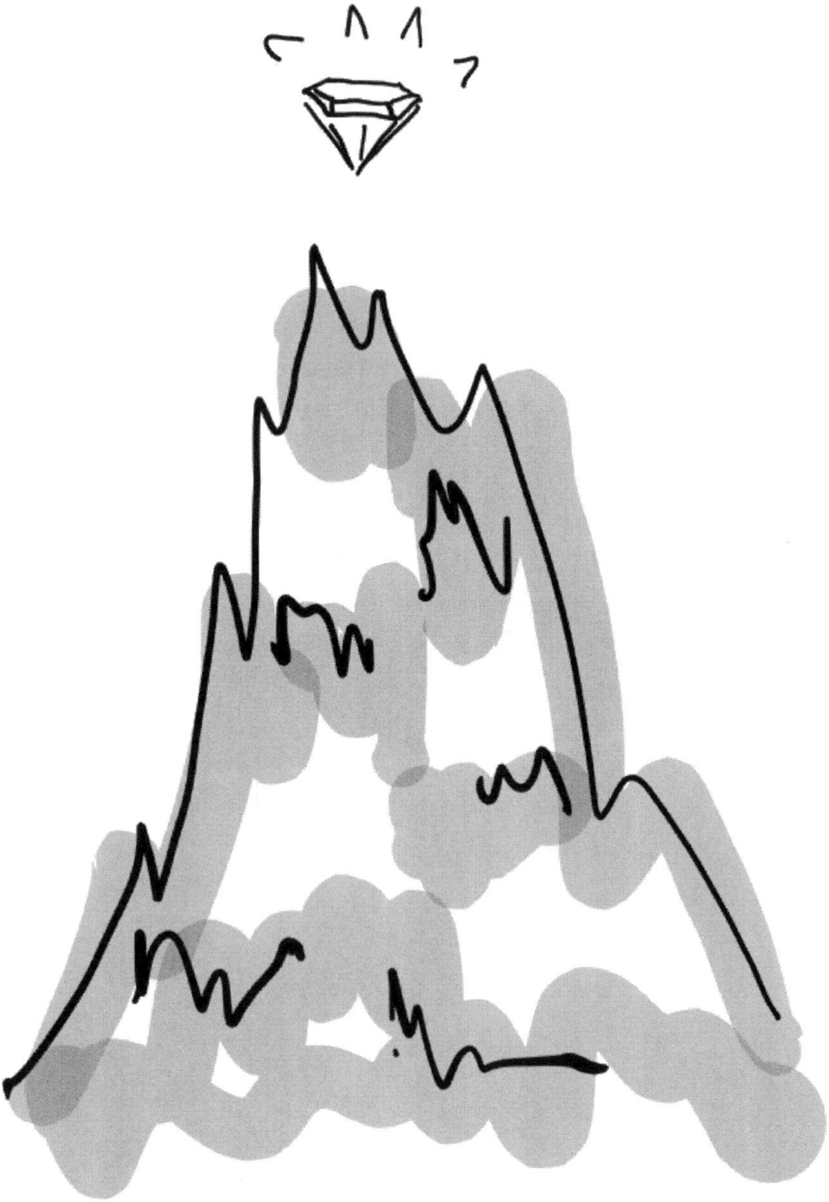

Chapter 8

HOW TO FIND YOUR ACTIONABLE BIG BRAND IDEA

> Don't confuse the logo or slogan for the brand.

The big idea is there. You may just not have uncovered it yet.

Whether you're starting from scratch or building on something that already has merit, the brand has to stand on its own—not just serve as a catchy slogan. It must be memorable and actionable.

SETTING A FRAMEWORK

"Brand" is that idea in someone's mind when they think of you. As a marketer and brander, it's your job to give them key elements to think about, relate to, and embrace. That's where your Purpose and the Brand Promise come in. That helps set the tone for everything else.

In a vacuum, people will come up with this on their own. As a marketing leader, it's your job to take a leadership role inside the institution and out in the marketplace to help craft a brand that's actionable and memorable.

The logo, color palette, name, tagline, graphics and photos—they are not your brand. Those are the elements that, over time, become shorthand for your brand story.

So as you explore rebranding or evolving, your first action is to zero in on Purpose and Promise. All the exercises in this section begin with research, strategy, and purpose.

> This Big Brand Idea must be both *authentic* (everyone can spot the posers right away, right?) and *aspirational*.

If you jump directly to a new logo, slogan, or other brand elements without the foundational exploration, your efforts will be nothing more than putting lipstick on that pig. They are destined to fail.

Let's DO SOMETHING.

This Big Brand Idea must be both authentic (everyone can spot the posers right away, right?) and aspirational.

STEP 1: RESEARCH

Research takes time and requires budget. But don't skip this step. It's foundational to learning where your unique strengths can help elevate and separate your institution from every other. This is where you find the AH-HAs!

Gather your team and discuss these questions.

Start by getting key input from C-suite and other involved stakeholders. With everyone around the table, have some in-depth discussion.

If you really want to get fancy, chart this out with 2 columns: current and desired.

Where did you come from? (History, why you started, your founding fathers/mothers…)

Where are you going? (What's your desired future state?)

What are the top 3-5 goals in your bank's business plan?

What is your current brand promise to customers?

In what concrete ways do you deliver on your brand promise to customers?

What is your current brand promise to employees?

In what concrete ways do you deliver on your brand promise to employees?

How would you describe your FI to someone who knows nothing about you?

What makes your FI better than competitors?

Where are you weak against competitors?

Describe your best customers:
- demographics
- psychographics
- their data profiles
- do other members of their family bank with you?

Who are your most difficult customers:
- demographics
- psychographics
- their data profiles
- do other members of their family bank with you?

Who are customers you could serve really well, but don't?

If your brand had a soundtrack, what kind of music would be on it?

If you sold coffee at your bank, what kind would it be? (For example: Starbucks, Folgers, local coffeehouse-style coffee, strong cup of joe, no coffee - we would have tea, kombucha, or something else).

What feeling/emotion/trait would you like to convey to customers? (add multiple choice list here)

What feeling/emotion/trait would you like to convey to employees?

If your brand had a celebrity spokesperson (living or dead) who would you want it to be?

If your brand was a vehicle, what would it be - and why?

What are some brands you admire (financial OR other sectors) and why?

One way to capture recurring themes—especially if you have a lot of people giving input—is to use AI to spot commonalities in the answers. Creating word clouds can also bring shared ideas to the forefront.

> What are the stories you tell about how you helped others with their financial needs? Whether it's retail, small business or commercial banking, trust services or others, there are stories about people realizing their dreams, beating the odds, building something new or getting a fresh start. Find them.

Look ahead.

How does the feedback from your first step align with your desired future state?

What would we need to change in terms of products, services, locations, technology, processes, people, philosophy, budgets, (fill in the blank) to get there?

Conduct a Self-Audit (Brand Psychoanalysis?)

Create a list of all the places your brand appears. Then evaluate each of them for messaging, clarity, consistency. Do they tell a story? Is it the right story?

Use these four Vs as a guide:

Visuals: Look for consistency of colors, fonts, photography styles, and logo use.

Voice: Copy should always reflect the brand personality. Avoid bank-speak.

Virtue: Your brand purpose and mission should shine throughout.

Value: Your point of differentiation, what you deliver. Why customers should choose your institution.

Your list should include (but not be limited to):

Social Media
- ads
- posts
- "about" copy
- hashtags

Print Media
- placed marketing/branding ads
- employment ads
- sponsorship ads: playbills, sports bills, church bulletins, school newsletters

Digital Media
- placed marketing/branding ads
- employment ads
- videos
- scripts

Collateral
- brochures (print and digital)
- flyers
- statement stuffers (print and digital)
- business cards
- notecards

Website
- blog
- social media links

- "about" copy
- employment information
- supplier and employee diversity statements

Internal Communications
- employee handbook
- intranet
- internal social media
- break room signage, amenities, environment
- shareholder communications and annual reports

Often Overlooked Communications
- after-hours phone greetings (corporate and individuals)
- on-hold music or messages
- email signatures
- virtual meeting backgrounds
- media sponsorship scripts such as "weather brought to you by..."
- drive-up: window signs, teller notices, back-of-house info
- ATM signage and screen graphics
- marquee messages and graphics
- parking lots
- reception area graphics, furnishings, and signage
- restroom graphics, amenities, and signage
- name tags

- corporate apparel and dress code
- fleet graphics
- special event signage
- sponsored event banners
- corporate swag

This audit will reveal a lot about how others perceive the brand.

Conduct employee listening

Focus group input is qualitative, not quantitative. But it can raise red flags and bring some AH-HA! moments when you listen.

Employee Focus Groups

Find out:

- why they're there
- what they love
- what they dislike
- what they wish they could tell you or get from you
- what they need that they're not getting
- what they tell other people
- what they think customers feel and believe
- what they think the community feels and believes
- what they think about the bank's competitors

Online Employment Reviews
Hear:

- what they liked about leadership
- their thoughts on culture
- what they say about how they were treated

Employee Exit Interview Documents

- Your bank does conduct those, right?

Employee Comments on Social Media and Intranet
You could be surprised.

If your FI has conducted employee culture or satisfaction surveys, review this information.
Some repeat these ever year or every two years. Look for trends.

Observe what's happening in your physical branches: inside, at the drive-up, and at ATMs.

Conduct customer research
Use a combination of surveys, focus groups, and one-on-one interviews.

Listen

Find out:

- why they're there
- what they love
- what they dislike
- what they wish they could tell you or get from you
- what they need that they're not getting
- what they tell other people
- what they think customers feel and believe
- what they think the community feels and believes
- what they think about the bank's competitors

Customer Focus Groups

Find out why they're there. What they love, what they dislike. What they wish they could get from you or tell you. What do they need that they're not getting. What they tell other people.

Customer Surveys

Here's where you can gain quantitative feedback if you generate enough responses. This can be very helpful if you're trying to predict a similar answer or feeling across your entire customer base.

Online Customer Comments

What are people saying on the channels you own? Facebook, LinkedIn and the others you manage can be telling. Are you just putting content out there, or are people engaging with you?

Don't forget about other review sites where people can leave ratings and reviews such as your Google business page, Yelp!, and Bankrate. Google yourself and find all the places your name appears. You may be surprised.

Claim and populate the pages you have the ability to affect. Read and absorb what people are saying.

Be wary of influencing the research

Flawed research can become like a brand's worst echo chamber: marketers hear only the things they want to hear and don't even realize that it's happening. That means decision-making about major initiatives like product changes and service offerings could result in very costly mistakes.

Customers, on the other hand, can feel frustrated and alienated. "You took the time to ask me," they think. "But you didn't listen." That sends a message—whether you meant it or not—that you don't care.

Four ways to make sure your research delivers the truth

If you really are looking for reliable feedback to help your brand improve products and customer experience, build these four best practices into your research:

1. Don't design the questions yourself

Engage a professional to design the survey instruments and the questions. A third party with the proper training will frame questions in a neutral manner to help you avoid unintentional bias that can result from being too close to the topics, as well as that which can come from cultural and background-related experiences of the respondents.

For example, using a term like "holiday spending" in a survey thinking it only refers to Christmas and Hanukkah excludes audiences who celebrate gift-giving holidays at different times and for different reasons. Western-sounding names and generationally familiar terms like Rolodex can also create confusion or inaccurate responses.

2. Test every survey every time

Just because it makes sense to you does not mean it makes sense to the people you want to listen to. Run some tests to find out whether the questions are clear and make sense. Be certain respondents get to convey what they want to say. Make sure they're not confused about what you're asking.

Be sure they can tell you what you really need to hear.

3. Use multiple feedback channels

Don't rely solely on a single research instrument to make major decisions; you may not have gone deep enough. Surveys combined with focus groups, social listening, interviews, or other methods can yield better, more insightful results.

4. Consider collaborating with different departments

Involve others in the organization when developing research and again when analyzing results. The different perspectives of colleagues may bring light and nuance to issues that you didn't notice. This will reduce the risk of making assumptions that steer you in the wrong direction. You'll also build alliances that can help you move your new branding or other initiatives forward.

STEP 2. REVIEW/RENEW THE MISSION AND PURPOSE

Mission, purpose, vision—oh, and those core values—definitely need your review. They might also need a freshen up or complete overhaul.

What are you really here to do?

The banks that know with certainty what they're here to do can truly be different. Some of our favorites boiled down to a very easy-to-remember and share statement are:

- Financial health for all
- Growing the local economy
- Building the entrepreneurship that's the backbone of America

Fast, local loan decisions and great customer service are not your brand or your why. Those are simply byproducts of your offerings.

Look to some well-known consumer brands for inspiration:

> **How do these apply to employees as well as customers?**

Marines

"Marines are trained to improvise, adapt and overcome any obstacle in whatever situation they are needed. They have the willingness to engage and the determination to defeat the enemy until victory is seized." — U.S. Marine Corps

Sony

"To be a company that inspires and fulfills your curiosity."

Walmart
"We save people money so they can live better."

Lego
"To inspire and develop the builders of tomorrow."

Once you really know your purpose, decision-making about marketing strategies and tactics becomes much easier because you can readily discard ideas that don't support your positioning.

Your purpose/mission must be better

This *isn't* a boring, lengthy, and forgettable mission statement. This is about why you are here.

I'll say that again. It is WHY you are here. If you haven't figured that out yet, it merits time for deep thinking and analysis. It probably requires more than a pinch of boldness; diplomatically questioning and challenging the status quo inside your financial institution isn't easy. But it's important if you want to make progress.

> Many mission statements are far too wordy. They're not unique or memorable. Ask someone in your organization. Can they recall the mission statement without looking it up?

Your mission statement may be a very sensitive issue.

The selection of mission statements below are real-life examples.

Weak mission statements

Statement: "We're committed to putting our customers, colleagues, communities and shareholders first, because when they succeed, we succeed."

Negative: Everyone is "first." That makes no sense.

Statement: "Our mission is to be the premier community banking institution providing financial services for our market, by surpassing customer's expectations and fulfilling community needs in a manner that enhances value."

Negative: This does not differentiate much. Enhances value to whom?

Statement: "We work to meet our customers' business and personal banking needs with competitive products and services, convenient access to their accounts, and proven stability backed by industry-leading financial metrics."

Negative: This is a commodity position.

Strong mission statements

Statement: "We are committed to improving the quality of life in the communities we serve by making positive financial, social, and environmental impacts. We intentionally build opportunities and pathways to success for the underrepresented members of our community."

Positive: Specific about the positive outcomes of their work and the people they serve.

Statement: "Help our customers succeed by bringing ingenuity, simplicity, and humanity to banking. At Capital One, we're changing banking for good. We were founded on the belief that no one should be locked out of the financial system."

Positive: Emotional and inclusive while talking about making finance easy and accessible.

> I repeat, What are you really here to do? Don't you dare say it's great customer service.

Statement: "Reimagine finance as a force for good and become the most impactful bank contributing to the drawdown of atmospheric CO2."

Positive: Bold, specific, emotional, positive, and aspirational.

The banks that have their purpose figured out and articulated are leaps ahead of their competition.

Once you really know your purpose, decision-making about marketing strategies and tactics becomes much easier because you can readily discard ideas that don't support your positioning and your WHY.

STEP 3. COMPOSE AUDIENCE PERSONAS

Who Are You Here to Serve?

Refer to the research you completed. (Please don't tell me you've skipped this step.) Look at what you uncovered about people you currently serve really well and the people you desire to serve really well with financial solutions that yield long-term relationships.

List them.

Divide them into groups based on shared characteristics.

Sketch out defining characteristics of each segment (e.g., demographics, behaviors, needs).

Develop detailed persona profiles.

For each segment, develop fictional (yet realistic) characters representing the ideal customers that match your bank's purpose. Think about them as people, not a faceless mass.

Give each character a name and a picture.

Include key information about "Sally," "Jameel," and "Mara" such as:

- Demographics (age, gender, location, income, education)
- Psychographics (lifestyle, interests, values, attitudes)
- Behaviors (online habits, purchasing patterns, media consumption)
- Goals and challenges (what they want to achieve, obstacles they face)
- Pain points (frustrations and problems)
- Motivations (what drives their decisions)
- Buyer journey (decision-making process)

Think about them as real people. Describe:

- What they care about
- What their normal day is like

- Where you find them
- How your institution might answer their needs.

Remember that you are not for everyone. No bank has enough resources of time, talent, or money to reach everyone. Pursue the people you can best serve.

Evaluate and rank them. You may have just identified numerous "ideal customers." The problem is, your marketing budget probably isn't large enough, nor your marketing team person-power deep enough to effectively reach all the audiences you've just detailed.

Now is the time to narrow down to a top few audience groups. Next, prioritize them: 1-2-3 to help consider the percent of resources you'll allot to marketing to them.

Establish a rank for each, then assign marketing budget proportionately. This takes discipline. It can be hard to let go of an audience, even if it becomes evident that they're a losing proposition. But basing the decisions on hard numbers will help your marketing spend go further.

Prioritizing helps you select the top audiences most likely to buy and concentrate your marketing efforts there. This allows you to build the reach and frequency that put your brand on the radar of the people most important to you.

You may want to do some testing with an audience to determine if it represents opportunity for your brand. That's OK. But do it wisely, establish a testing budget up front rather than stealing budget from other audiences later. That's a risk that may not pay off.

Martha Bartlett Piland, CFMP

Sample Customer Persona Graphic

B🔶NKTASTIC®

sample customer persona: MILLENNIAL BUSINESS OWNER "Ariel"

BIO
Ariel is a millennial owner/founder of a clicks and mortar women's boutique. She's in early stages of business and has been so successful that she's soon launching another specialty boutique.

Her business has grown rapidly. Her husband Jim has quit his corporate job to be a stay-at-home dad for their children who are home schooled.

She is very interested in supporting other women entrepreneurs and uses her influence to help them.

age: 36
status: married + 5 children
location: Wichita, KS
education: BA Communications
philosophy: quality vs. quantity

PERSONALITY
- Perennially positive and sunny.
- Risk-taker.
- Includer; she makes women feel like they are part of her gang.
- Mentor: she wants young girls to grow up with a positive, can-do attitude like hers.

BIGGEST PAIN POINT
"I wish my bank acted like they cared about me and my business, not just making money off of me. Honestly, I'd switch to a different bank if it didn't feel so overwhelming."

PRIORITIES
- 16% growth
- 26% save time
- 37% family
- 21% profit

GOALS & DREAMS
- Grow another successful business.
- Be a significant part of her kids' lives.
- Save time and money so she can 'do it all.'
- Better manage her cash and her businesses; be more capable with the finance side of her work.

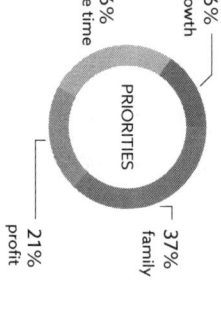

BUSINESS PROFILE
annual sales: $1.2 million
employees: 2 FTEs • 6 PTEs
years in business: 6
banking relationships: 7 (3 personal and 4 business)

PREFERRED BANKING METHOD
"The best of both worlds.... I need to bank on my phone, but I also want a real person who can help me make the most of my businesses."

COMMUNICATIONS
- Instagram and Facebook are her predominant social channels.
- To get her attention immediately, TEXT or use Messenger.
- She uses very little email to receive communications, though she uses email heavily with her customers.

Audience Personas for Employees Are Equally Important

Brand alignment is vitally important. It means developing an inseparably linked employer brand with your externally facing brand.

Without it, you risk looking like a wannabe bank. When everything's aligned, employees embrace it. Customers feel it. That's the foundation of deep and loyal relationships.

If you already thought of that, bonus point for you. If not, then it's essential to consider employees—likely in different segments—as important audiences with personas as well.

This will make a difference in your culture and employer brand because employees won't be an afterthought. They'll be included in these foundational planning efforts.

Whether you need more customer-facing staffers, more back-of-house people, or need to deepen your bench to support impending senior leadership retirements, taking the time for this step will set you up for success.

Huntington Bank's website https://huntington-careers.com/ talks about bringing your authentic self to work. They are very focused on inclusion of all people. Their corporate internal brand has garnered numerous awards.

"Welcome to careers at Huntington. Be a part of how we look out for people.

It's obvious you're the kind of person who's going places, and Huntington is going places, too. It seems we naturally attract people who share our can-do attitude, service heart, and forward-thinking perspective. We care about the community and the people on our team. We're confident and excited about how we can succeed together. We'd love to have you join us."

Sample Employee Persona Graphic

B⁂NKTASTIC®

sample employee persona: GEN Z LENDER "Carlos"

BIO
Carlos is a 23-year-old Gen Z man who recently graduated from a local university with a business degree.

He joined the bank because he has a passion for financial literacy and equity for underrepresented minority communities.

He carries a small amount of college student debt.

Carlos' family is very important. And though they live in another state, they maintain close ties.

age: 23
status: single
location: Boise, ID
education: BA Business
voted: most likely to succeed

PERSONALITY
- Positive and ambitious.
- Can talk to anyone.
- Generous with praise, and conservative with spending.
- Always learning.
- Values tech and values people.

PURPOSE
"I want to work in a bank with people who make a difference in the community, especially for those who have traditionally been under banked or unbanked. At the end of the day, I ask, 'who have I helped?'"

PRIORITIES
- 25% investing
- 30% career
- 25% family
- 20% friends

GOALS & DREAMS
- Personal goal of real estate investing for future income streams.
- Wants a career mentor to help him grow his skills and his worth to others.
- Be promoted to a well-regarded lending officer, then a market president.

EMPLOYEE PROFILE
years with the bank: 1
employment history: internships only
commute: 30 minutes each way
location: mid-town branch • WFH 1 day/week
volunteers: Junior Achievement

WORKING STYLE
Face-to-face interactions supported by phone calls and emails—tailored to customer preference.

COMMUNICATIONS
- Snapchat and TikTok are his predominant social channels.
- He prefers to communicate via TEXT.
- He uses very little email to receive communications, though he uses email heavily with customers and prospects.

Sample Vision Board

Photo credits: Curated Lifestyle, Diaga Ellaby, Faruk Toklougul, Getty Images, Hans Isaacson, Heather Ford, Henley Design Studio, Jessica Johnston, Joel Muniz, Joshua Fernandez, Kateryna Hliznitsova, Maddi Bazzocco, Mark Stosberg, Patrycja Jadach, Randy Tarampi, The Nix Company, and Valentina Conde-all on unsplash.com

> Compliance officers are your friends. It is imperative that when you're developing personas, you are ethically determining and defining the people you will serve.

Design Visual Representations of Your Audience Personas

Creating visual representations of real people in your audience (not just numbers) will help your team develop campaign communications that resonate.

An effective way to build these visuals of your personas is to make vision boards for each person. As a team, comb through lifestyle and business magazines and blogs. Peruse the social media channels they might use and note images that fit. Look for quotes and headlines that represent the individuals you have in mind. You should also think about the music the personas would like, the books they'd read, and the activities they choose.

Take about 45 minutes to assemble these ideas, then share, compare, edit, curate, and select. Then assemble them into collages. These can be digital or paper collages.

Some teams find it convenient to create these vision boards on a private Pinterest page. This approach lets you edit and add to your vision boards as you learn more about these audiences.

Now that you have strong visual representations of the audiences you want to serve, you will want to make sure the personas and vision boards are readily available for internal

> Word of caution: They may not like you.

reference when creating products, content, messaging, social media posts—everything.

"Mara" may not be like you. Don't assume that she is. Assumptions can take you way off course. Charles LeFevre, Founder and Principal Consultant at Stanford Hill, advises bankers to take time and observe. "Go, sit in the seat in the lobby and look around. What does it look like from the customer's perspective?"

Charles says we're quick to miss things and become blinded by the tactics. "We sometimes forget to look around and say, 'What is the customer seeing? How is the customer experiencing this? What else do I need to deliver to make sure that they're successful like that?'"

He advises that you do it constantly—never stopping. "Otherwise our brand will not be as effective. We won't be able to deliver on our mission because we've forgotten the core of it, which is that person we're trying to serve."

Chapter 9

SETTING THE STAGE FOR PRODUCTIVE, WOW-FILLED BRAINSTORMING EVENTS

Often, someone calls a brainstorm session and seats everyone around a table. The circle of people stare uncomfortably at each other. Some eventually start talking. Others never say a word. It's hard to get rolling.

The words "let's brainstorm," can feel as demoralizing as the words "root canal."

Let's change that.

Abide by the Ground Rules

Make it safe for people to put their ideas out there without self-editing. When you set that tone for every meeting—not just "brainstorming meetings"—you create an environment where employees feel comfortable expressing new ideas. When they're thinking out loud and challenging the status quo without fear of judgment or ridicule, magic happens.

Model and encourage open communication, active listening, and respectful feedback to promote a sense of trust and psychological safety. Adopt rules everyone must follow:

- always state the goal up front
- no criticism allowed
- never kill an idea — work to make it better
- no one is allowed to say "that won't work" or "it didn't work before"
- quantity counts: the more ideas generated, the better
- don't fall in love with the first idea, always measure back against the original goal

Structure Brainstorming Gatherings Differently

Change the mental construct. Don't call them meetings and don't make them feel like meetings. Instead, think of your brainstorming sessions as gatherings or events.

Warm Up

Always start with an icebreaker. A rapid-fire round of charades or a two-minute race sculpting animals from Play-Doh will free up thinking and ignite group energy. This is time well spent.

Engage the Senses

When we attend an event—like a party or a wedding, or even a funeral—many pieces come together to engage all our senses. Strive to bring sight, sound, touch, smell, and taste into your brainstorming events. It fires up more areas of the brain and enlivens creativity.

Here are ways to bring sensory engagement for your participants:

- share healthy treats or retro candy like Pop Rocks that conjures up childhood memories
- crank up an energizing music playlist
- invite participants to wear hats or jerseys from their favorite teams
- provide colored felt-tip markers or colored pencils to use instead of standard pens

Get Physical

Brainstorm standing up or while playing musical chairs. Try sitting on the floor on huge fluffy pillows or bean bag chairs. Or offsite axe throwing. Experiment at a picnic table in a park or some other outdoor location. Or simply with a group walk around the block.

Breaking old habits and moving around is a team builder that invites new ideas to flow.

> Don't just call a brainstorming session. Give it a lot more ooomph! with creative exercises.

Once the basics are set, use some prescribed exercises to spur different ways of thinking. Following are three that we've developed.

Brainstorm Exercise: We're on a Mission from God

The Blues Brothers Jake and Elwood knew what they were about: to raise $5,000 to pay a delinquent tax bill for the Catholic orphanage that reared them.

When was the last time you reviewed your mission and vision statements? Can you remember them? Do they make your heart beat faster? Does your team know them?

Write down the current mission.

How could you restate your mission from other points of view?

Inc. Magazine once highlighted ShowMe Tickets, reporting their mission "appears to have been translated from the original Klingon: '*We unite behind a common purpose greater than work itself—crush the competition.... We will dominate any industry we choose.*'"

It's still one of our favorites.

Observe and gain inspiration from others to give your mission statement a fresh jolt of energy. How could the voices of other characters or people inspire yours to be—well—more inspiring?

- James Bond
- The United States Marines
- Oscar the Grouch
- The Peace Corps
- Patrick Mahomes
- Winnie the Pooh
- Oprah
- Sir Richard Branson
- Winston Churchill
- Steve Jobs
- My Little Pony
- Barbie
- Taylor Swift
- Ser Davos
- The Tooth Fairy
- Ted Lasso
- Spider Man

STEP 4. CREATIVE DEVELOPMENT

Creative development can feel fun and exciting. Sometimes it feels daunting or chaotic.

Consistently implementing an A-B-C creative process—every time—builds marketing muscle. A focused, strategic approach can ensure that the creative work reaches its intended audience and achieves the desired results.

Whether you're developing creative campaign internally or working with an external bank marketing agency, these steps will help your team be on the same page, stay on track, and produce effective work.

A. Always Start with a Creative Strategy Brief

Before diving into the creative development process, establish a strategy brief. This document should outline your goals, objectives, strategies, tactics, and target audience. By insisting on a written document, you ensure that everyone involved is on the same page.

The brief should also describe other aspects of the situation and how you're trying to solve it. Stipulate such things as tone, brand non-negotiables, and any compliance requirements.

Dig deeper into describing the target audience. Delve into the personas with them so your team understands their daily life, worries, excitements, and potential needs that your institution can fulfill.

> Whether working with an internal team or an external bank marketing agency, always insist on starting with a brief before creating, evaluating and testing. Not only does it ensure the work is on-strategy, it also reduces the risk of wheel spinning, wasted budget, and potential damage to your brand reputation.

Identify where you can find these people and make sure the ideas you're developing will meet them where they are. Whether working with an internal team or an external bank marketing agency, always insist on starting with a brief before creating, evaluating and testing. Not only does it ensure the work is on-strategy, it also reduces the risk of wheel spinning, wasted budget, and potential damage to your brand reputation.

B. Brainstorm the Creative Concepts

Once you have a clear and comprehensive strategy brief in place, it's time to let your imagination go wild. This is the fun part where you can banter with your team and come up with a large number of concepts and themes. Make it fun. Dare to be stupid. Work with a goal of coming up with as many ideas as possible. The more, the better.

When you're brainstorming, it's important to give every idea a chance. Not every idea will be right for your specific goals and target audience. But that's OK. Don't cut anything right away. Get it all on the table.

Too many great ideas are killed by self-editing or the Donnie Downers who say "that will never work" or "we tried that before already." In this phase, generate a multitude of ideas without criticism or editing.

It's easy to fall in love with the first idea or get carried away with a wildly cool concept. So *after* the brainstorming session is the time to evaluate.

C. Curate the Concepts

One of the most difficult things to do in this process is to objectively evaluate the work. You're very close to this assignment. You may be in love with some of your ideas. Of course you are, you've worked hard on this.

Make the First Cuts

This requires critical thinking and discipline. Take what you think are your top 2-3 ideas and measure them one by one against the strategy brief. Take the time to measure each idea that you think may have merit against the criteria in your brief.

They must fulfill the goals you outlined in that document. If they don't, then save them for another day—but not now.

- Ask yourself if the idea effectively communicates your message to the target audience.
- Does it align with their needs and desires?
- Does it fit within your brand's tone and values?
- Is it truly unique?
- Is it clear and memorable?

By examining each idea against the established criteria, you can identify the strongest concepts that are most likely to support your goals. You may be astonished to find that your favorite ideas don't actually pull their weight. You might have to "kill your darlings."

> Remember it's the target audience whom your brand must appeal to. Not you.

The phrase "Kill your darlings" has been attributed to William Faulkner, Stephen King, and other writers. It essentially means to eliminate or significantly revise parts of your work that don't serve the purpose of the story you're trying to tell... even if you're particularly in love with them. It means being ruthless. And while that phrase is meant for literary works, it applies extremely well to telling your brand story.

That means you may need to take another look at some of the runner-up ideas. Or, it could mean you have more work to do.

You will do additional evaluation and research. But this helps you narrow down the ideas that should make the first cut.

Brainstorm Exercise: Tennessee Round Table

(Time frame: 20+ minutes)

Rumor has it that Tennessee Williams worked on multiple plays at once by having multiple typewriters around his dining room table.

He'd work on one until he was out of ideas, then move to another seat at another typewriter and begin working on the play that was underway there. Rather than allowing himself to get stuck and stop working altogether, he kept moving. He was a prolific, award-winning writer. You know the rest.

Your assignment: raid the supply room for a stack of note pads and colored pencils and pens. Write a challenge you're working on at the top of each note pad. (Go for 7 or more if you can.) Find a conference room with a big table and place the note pads in different spots in front of the chairs.

> This exercise works well for small group sessions. Be sure to have 2-3 more notepads than participants to avoid bottlenecks. Some people are faster than others, so this will keep the ideas flowing.

Break out the colored pencils and place one in front of each notebook. At the top of the first page in each book or pad:
1. State the assignment.
2. State the goals or outcomes desired.
3. Begin writing possible ideas/solutions in your first book or note pad. No editing, just write and let it flow.
4. When you run out of ideas, move to the next problem and start on it.

Brainstorm Exercise: Turn It Upside Down

(Time frame: 65 minutes… or more)

Innovation comes from dumping out the box and starting fresh. Even the tiniest assumptions—when upended—can turn into something magical.

case in point: Marc Jacobs at Fashion Week

ASSUMPTION: a fashion show must be in a hall on a stage.

Producers at Marc Jacobs set up their show on a sidewalk instead. It put more spotlight on the clothes and less attention on the props. It also moved them away from competitors... and probably saved a fortune on venue rental.

case in point: Lewis Miller florals as public art
ASSUMPTION: outdoor trash cans are for trash.
New York floral designer Lewis Miller used city trash cans as over-sized vases for pop-up arrangements all over Manhattan. Awe-inspiring work that embraces tourists and locals is also a PR magnet. Read one of many stories about it (with photos) here: on.today.com/4gXDZNb

What boxes of assumptions do you need to dump out?

SITUATION	ASSUMPTION	ALTERNATIVE
Customers only want:		
Our annual report must:		
Talent recruitment always:		

Now that you've taken a look at some of your assumptions, take a look at some of your processes. Do they need to be dumped out and reimagined?

- new business/sales process
- customer experience

- employee onboarding
- employee exiting
- supplier communications
- new product development

Choose one to diagram how you do it now. Then upend the box. Sketch out an alternative that could positively flow to your bottom line. (Put a date on your calendar to work on the others.)

How will we know if this is a good idea?

How will we test these ideas?

STEP 5. EVALUATE AND TRY IT ON FOR SIZE

By now, you have landed on some concepts that fulfill the requirements of your strategy brief. Let's investigate further to determine what can hold up to scrutiny under many conditions.

Sketch out the answers to more questions below:

The Concept

Can it be both authentic and aspirational?

Will it deliver value to the bank? How?

Will it deliver value to customers? How?

Does it stand up to a Google search to see if anyone else is using it, or if it may have a negative meaning?

Who else (if anyone) is doing this or something similar? How is our approach unique from others?

The Name

If you're incorporating a name change, does it stand up to a Google search?

Does the name stand up to a search with the US Patent & Trademark Office? (This is not the final OK. You still need legal counsel.)

Could it be misconstrued or come across as insensitive or offensive? How do you know?

Is there a URL and top level domains available with the name plus .com and .bank?

> Why do this? Only by strategically and thoroughly vetting all potential brand ideas can you demonstrate to leadership that supporting the change will help make the institution more successful.

If it's a manufactured/made up name, have you checked to be sure it doesn't have an alternate or negative meeting in another language?

The Slogan

Does it stand up to a Google search?

Does it stand up to a search with the US Patent & Trademark Office? uspto.gov (This is not the final OK. You still need legal counsel.)

Could it be misconstrued or come across as insensitive or offensive? How do you know?

STEP 6. DRAW YOUR LINE IN THE BRAND SAND

By now, you may have one clear winner. Or you may have a top two that seem most viable. Continue testing with potential scenarios.

With one or two top contenders, it's a good practice to sketch out how the brand could be brought to life in multiple ways. Following are two exercises to help you—and others in your institution—visualize the brand in action.

The Business Perspective

Does the bank currently have products that would fulfill this brand promise? What are they? If not, what would it take to make that happen?

Does the bank have services that would fulfill promise? What are they? If not, what would it ta tute them?

Would these products and services help the bank:

- attract new customers
- retain customers
- make more money

Would our team support and be excited to deliver on this brand? Do they have the:

- passion?
- bandwidth?
- training?

1. Interview your future brand: Imagine your Future Brand profiled in a news story or documentary by someone you admire such as Oprah, Sir Richard Branson, or Barbara Walters. How would your Future Brand complete these sentences?

When we were founded, our vision was _____.

Our vision has evolved to _____ because _____.

The person we most look up to is _____.

We love our mascot! He/she/they is _____.

Our most successful relationships are _____.

Three things we can't live without are _____.

The impact we make for our customers is _____
and here's an example of how we do it _____.

We define excellent customer experience as _____.

Our customer loyalty is _____.

When people tell their friends about us, they say
_____.

When the press wants to interview us, it's because _____.

The best advice we've ever gotten is _____.

The book we tell everyone to read is _____.

We never forget to _____.

2. Diagram your future brand(s): Recruit colleagues from other departments for help. Get out an array of markers and large sheets of paper or a whiteboard. Set a time frame and establish the purpose of the exercise with everyone.

Do a warm-up as outlined previously in Step 3.

If you're evaluating 2-3 concepts, then set up different white board areas for each. Allow enough room for people to walk around and write their thoughts in a free-flowing manner.

Write your proposed purpose/brand in the center of a circle.

> **Dare to be stupid. The goal of brainstorming is to generate as many ideas as possible without self-editing.**

One the left side of the diagram, write down ways this brand could be implemented with and for employees.

On the right side of the diagram, write down ways this brand could be put into action with and for customers.

In addition to words, people can add pictures, sketches, emojis—whatever it takes to get the ideas across.

Don't worry about getting everything right or perfect. Don't worry about leaving some things out. This won't be a comprehensive—or even practical—list. This exercise is designed to help you imagine and visualize the brand concept in action.

If loads of ideas flow, this shows the group is enthusiastic about the idea and can imagine many ways to put the brand into action. That helps forecast future success.

If ideas are slow to flow, keep at it.

If something comes up that you aren't crazy about, don't kick the idea to the curb immediately. This may just mean it's an "out there" idea that will take a bit more time to explore. But if, after due time is given to this exploration, it may just not be for you. Or may be for your bank at a later phase.

Note: This works best in person, but if distance is a barrier, this work can be done in Zoom.

The sample chart on the next page is to help you get a sense of the exercise and get started. Your charts will look quite different.

Action-Oriented Inspiration from a Theoretical Perspective

These example ideas are generated by our team to help spur your thinking.

A **next-gen bank** could:

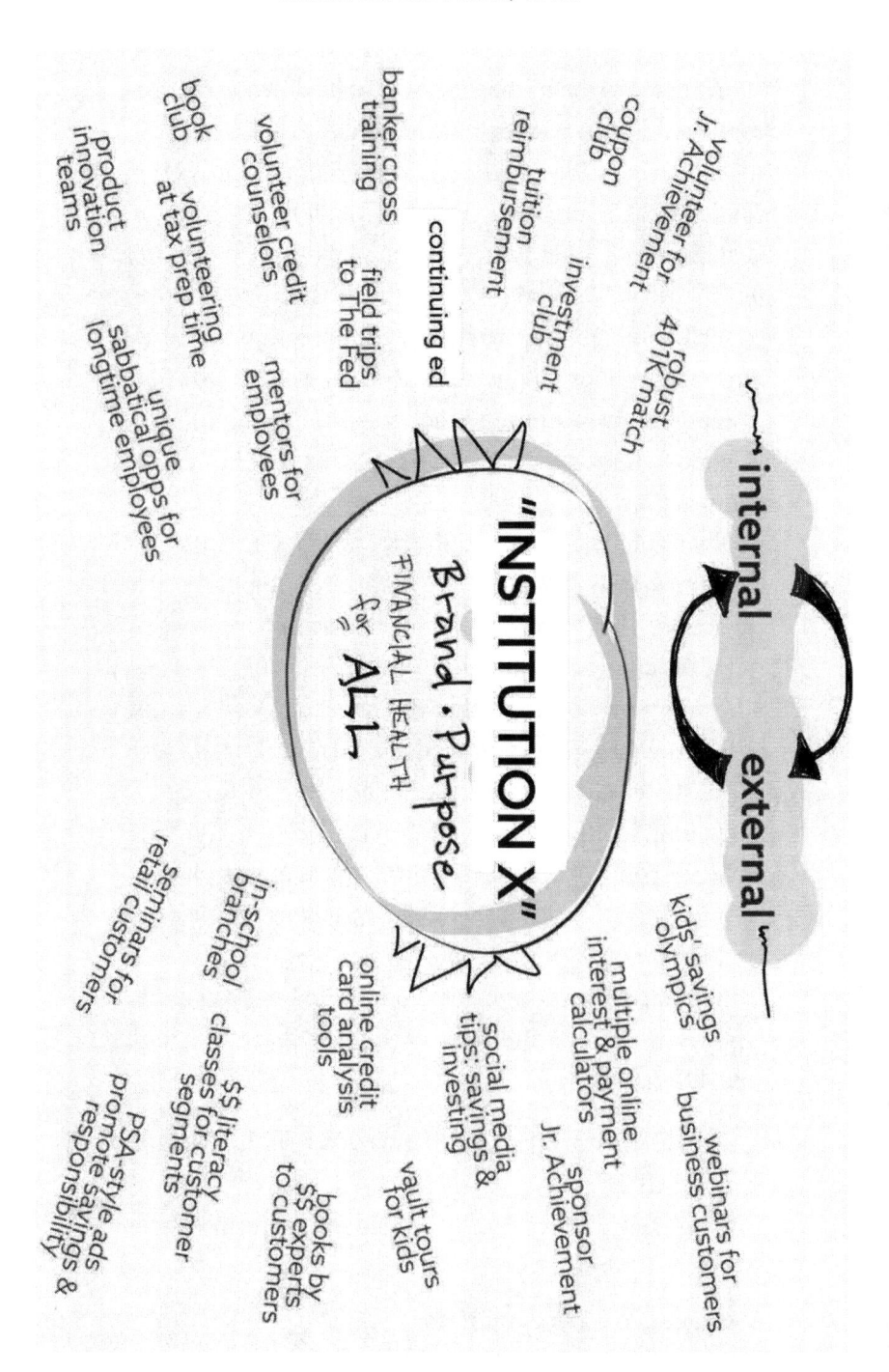

"INSTITUTION X"
Brand · Purpose
FINANCIAL HEALTH for ALL

internal ⇄ external

Internal:
- Jr. Achievement for Volunteer
- robust 401K match
- coupon club
- tuition reimbursement
- investment club
- banker cross training
- volunteer credit counselors
- continuing ed
- field trips to The Fed
- book club
- volunteering at tax prep time
- mentors for employees
- product innovation teams
- unique opps for sabbatical for longtime employees

External:
- kids' savings olympics
- webinars for business customers
- multiple online interest & payment calculators
- sponsor Jr. Achievement
- social media tips: savings & investing
- vault tours for kids
- online credit card analysis tools
- books by $$ experts to customers
- in-school branches
- $$ literacy classes for customer segments
- seminars for retail customers
- PSA-style ads promote savings & responsibility

- Assemble diverse advisory boards made up of people like their target customers instead of the "usual suspects."
- Provide an honorarium and business cards to board members.
- Develop new ways to connect young audiences with established community leaders for networking and mentoring.
- Partner with local colleges to offer banking services and financial ed to students.
- Hire cheerleaders from local teams to make appearances (and cheer) at customer ribbon cuttings and at bank special events.

A **high-experience brand** could:
- Give the customers with the most relationships a "skip the line" ticket to jump the line inside a branch or at the drive-through.
- Offer a VIP customer service phone number to call so there's never a long waiting queue.
- Offer a concierge to assist customers with other transactions such as booking restaurant reservations or event tickets.

A **luxury brand** might:
- Have high-end grooming products in the restrooms.
- Give business cards with unique/luxe materials to its bankers.

- Make in-person visits to customers with top-quality coffee in hand.

- Borrow a page from the airlines: offer a first-class lounge within branches where customers can relax, enjoy refreshments, and conduct their banking or other business in a more private and comfortable setting.

A brand focused on **local, small businesses** could:

- Pledge to purchase supplies and services only from local vendors.

- Support charities that keep their services and research local.

- Allow employees to volunteer on bank time to help local nonprofits.

- Offer meeting spaces to local nonprofit groups at no charge.

- Conduct webinars/seminars to help customers learn more about topics important to their business, such as social media, tax changes, marketing, and HR.

- Help minority- and women-owned small businesses gain SBA certifications.

A bank serving **faith communities** might:
- Construct specialized treasury management services for the Sunday collections.

- Offer armored car pick up of cash contributions on Sunday evenings.

- Adopt faith-based financial products that align with the values of the congregation, such as ethical investment options, faith-compliant loans, or savings accounts that support charitable giving.

- Foster volunteer grant programs where they donate funds to a congregation's charitable projects based on volunteer hours contributed by the congregation's membership.

A **green** or **environmentally conscious** brand could:
- Have a compost bin next to the trash and recycling bins outside.
- Invite people to recycle days in addition to shred days.
- Give business cards made of paper impregnated with seeds to plant.
- Offer employees a stipend for biking to work.
- Install bike racks outside for employees and customers.
- Sponsor or post ad messages on green public transportation.
- Instead of giving client gifts at Christmas, give gifts on Earth day.

Action-Oriented Inspiration from Other Institutions

Impressia Bank—since it's for women business owners—sends real-time text alerts about new business grant opportunities to its customers. They are also one of only two Profit-First affiliated financial institutions in the U.S. and use this expertise to help their customers be more profitable.

Her Bank hosts a motivational women's conference that highlights its business-owner customers and celebrates women in the community. The event is called "The Door to More."

From their website: Centered around "opening doors to new beginnings, growth, and transformation, it also allows us to close doors on what's no longer serving us. This idea of open and closed doors as it represents opportunity, choice, and transition inspired our event: Her Bank's 3 Year Celebration of Women, Wealth, and Wisdom."

Her Bank collaborated with local media, local small-business women, and others to deliver a very special event for their audiences.

Roger Bank is the digital military banking division of 122-year-old Citizens Bank of Edmond. It stands out with products and services that deliver on their promise to active military:

> One bank we've seen in Lawton, Oklahoma, has allocated a dedicated office in one of its branches to the CEO of a local nonprofit.

- "Round up" your savings plus Roger-matching funds to Round Up accounts.
- Early access to paycheck funds.
- No NSF fees, no overdraft fees, no minimum balance fees, no account maintenance fees.
- Recurring deposit setup and card locking for when people are deployed and off the grid.

Climate First Bank has special loan products for solar equipment and has expertise to discuss federal rebates and incentives with customers.

They also host live digital "fireside chats" that are later posted on their YouTube channel. Enticing titles like "Let's Talk Trash" and "Maximizing Solar Opportunities" highlight bank customers or experts in the space like Dr. Jane Goodall. They give viewers an in-depth view of the bank's mission and allow them to get a sense of whether they're a match.

An added benefit: These events offer tremendous increased visibility for those customers addressing climate change through their businesses or thought leadership.

Take Action: Engage All Senses

The most powerful brands engage not just sight and sound, but touch, smell, and even taste. Addressing all senses for your DO SOMETHING brand is a way to make your brand more memorable and attach to positive emotions.

It also makes your brand more inclusive because it offers more ways to interact with people who are disabled or differently abled.

Here are some examples to help spur your thinking:

Taste

If your brand is about:

strength - serve strong coffee or energy drinks

like family - serve homemade cookies

financial health - serve herbal tea, kombucha, or spring water

small business - serve treats from local bakeries or food manufacturers

These things relate to hospitality in a branch, but bankers who call on customers could bring these items with them for in-person meetings as well.

Client gifts could also be addressed in this manner. Instead of sending the traditional turkeys at holiday time, curate gift baskets with food and beverage items such as local honey, smoked cheeses, or produce items that support your brand position.

Smell

Play-Doh has that smell that transports us back to kindergarten. Movie theaters have that incredible buttery popcorn smell that greets patrons as soon as they walk through the door. And Victoria's Secret has a signature scent that wafts through its stores.

> When People's Bank activated its Banking UNusual campaign, its signature fragrance was the delicious smell of cookies baking in the lobby.

Bankers can borrow from this strategy too. Retail scent machines are a real thing and might be a good fit for your brand since scent can conjure up a wealth of feelings such as health, relaxation, or energy.

Sound

Besides advertising jingles, there are many other ways music and sound are used to build brands. Sound effects like the Playstation "wah" and the musical tone Microsoft makes are subtle but powerful branding cues that are reinforced many times over.

Branders should design their brand touchpoints with sound in mind. Areas to consider include:

- **Call centers** should have appropriate wait-time music and promotional recordings while customers are on hold. Do not use the same stock music used by thousands of competitors.

- **Voice mail greetings** can include music and a standardized voice mail script that incorporates your tagline.

- **Lobby sounds** should fit the vibe of your brand, whether that's music, pink noise, a TV with the stock market report, or the sound of last night's high school football game.

- **Website and social media** may be other places a branded sound can be used.

Her Bank by Legends Bank has taken the sound element seriously. It has curated two playlists on Spotify: one is a female-oriented holiday playlist, the other is a feel-good selection of songs by women, for women. Titles include "Woman Up" by Meghan Trainor, "Free Woman" by Lady Gaga, and "Girl on Fire" by Alicia Keys.

Her Bank has also started a podcast called InspirHER'd.

> For a really "out there" idea, you could have scratch-off business cards that reveal a QR code.

Touch

The cover of *Fast Company* magazine has an unusual texture. Pick it up in the dark and you'll immediately be able to identify it. Some consumer-packaged goods also do this brilliantly. Eco-conscious brands often package their products in uncoated, raw-textured paper, for example.

How can you translate this concept to your financial brand?

- **Die cut shapes or textured paper** could be used for business cards or collateral materials.
- **Handshakes**—do all your people know how to shake hands properly? Maybe you have a "secret handshake" for internal culture building.
- **Reception area furniture** should also have your personal (branded) touch.

Sight

Sight is the one people typically think of first because it includes the logo, color palette, and graphics package. It feels easy. But serious branders take it seriously. Besides the usual brand elements, also audit and design anything that an employee or customer will see.

Don't overlook:

- outdoor signage
- logo'd interior items like door mats, lobby posters, and ATM graphics
- employee name tags
- branded apparel
- fleet graphics
- sponsorship banners

Make sure your lobbies and drive-through areas look bright, clean, and fresh.

Get rid of sick plants or dusty silk arrangements. If your brand is about being green, do furnishings and supplies reflect that?

Get creative! What about branded graphics in the employee break room or in the parking lot? If the fit is right, take a cue from savvy retailers and use special lighting or floor graphics. Or even build retail displays in the lobby to represent how you help customers fulfill their dreams of homes, vacations, education, and more.

This could be a good time to conduct testing with your audiences.

While no research is 100 percent reliable, it can be a good step in your due diligence. Remember: you're very close to this assignment. What makes perfect sense to you can be lost on others.

> Since focus groups are not quantitative, remember that even if 90 percent of your focus group participants love your new brand idea, that does not assure you that 90 percent of all people will love it.

Test With Focus Groups

Focus groups are a good tool for listening and uncovering something that's potentially confusing, unclear, or offensive. And for raising additional questions.

These sessions can uncover feelings and emotions more easily than a survey. They also allow you to share visuals of creative concepts within the group and generate discussion around them.

Ideally, your focus groups are conducted by an outside professional. It's very difficult to be objective in these conversations if you're the one also leading the creative process. Because you'll have some favorites, that may sway you to pose questions and analyze answers in a way that favors your preferred choice.

Listen, then listen some more. You want to find out:

- Does the target audience grasp the value of what you're offering?

- Do the ideas evoke the desired emotions, such as humor, warmth, reassurance, or excitement?

- Does the message compel the action you seek?

- Is there any "finance speak" that makes sense to you, but not to your customer or prospect?

This feedback will help you refine and hone your concepts before moving forward with the campaign.

Since focus groups are not quantitative, remember that even if 90 percent of your focus group participants love your new brand idea, that does not assure you that 90 percent of all people will love it.

Test With a Survey

If budget permits, a survey can take you deeper into evaluation territory. Now is where you really can ascertain whether a majority of your audience likes and embraces your brand concept.

A well-crafted survey can also offer insights into some new product offerings and how those might be received by your audience. It can also give more intel about some of the actions you sketched out in Step 4.

Chapter 10

PUTTING YOUR BRAND INTO ACTION

By now, you have a clear-cut, 30,000-foot view of the direction for your action-oriented brand. Next, it's time to get detailed—into the weeds—on how you will execute on this brand promise for employees and for customers.

As your team conceptualizes these actions, it's vital that you dig deep and wide to unearth the potential actions that bring your special brand uniquely to life for your employees and for your customers.

It may still feel foreign to think about your brand in this way. You may want to revisit earlier examples to get you and your team in the right frame of mind.

You should also refer to the brainstorming activities in this book to help you think in an expansive, no-holds-barred way. You can always go back and edit things out later. As Doug Hall from Eureka! Ranch says, "The virtual NO kills more great ideas than anything else."

> If you want a break-out brand, you need break-out thinking.

Remember the Personas

Using your in-depth descriptions of your audience(s), you're ready to start creating ACTIONS that will reach them and appeal to them.

If those personas aren't fully fleshed-out, then take the time to fill in the details before going further.

Articulate What You Won't Do

When you're devising all the ways you will put your brand into action, you're probably designing things you *will* do.

Many banks and credit unions spend a lot of time saying what they will do:

- We will be the best.

- We will deliver excellent service.

> It can be very powerful to state what you *won't* do.

What won't you do?

This is critically important and can help guide everyone's actions in the organization. Consider a variety of "won't" promises such as:

- We won't take _____ for an answer.

- We won't cut corners or _____.

- We won't just tell people _____.

- We won't tolerate a culture of _____.

Because those are action steps, too.

STEP 7. FLESH OUT YOUR BRAND ACTIVATION BLUEPRINT

Refer to the diagram of the winning concept you formulated with your team during brainstorming.

Now is the time to chart a comprehensive map of all the ways this brand can be put into action. Look at the previous ideas again and start there.

It may help to make a visual sketch of the strategies and tactics already in place and identify them as "existing" in a certain color. When you write down what's already happening, it becomes easier to see the areas that are out of balance.

As you did in the first level of this exercise, think broadly and expansively. Don't self-edit yet. Get on paper as many ideas as you can that support putting this brand concept into action.

An effective method is to put large sheets of paper on the walls where you're meeting. Put the titles for key areas such as Customer Experience, Hiring, etc. at the top of each.

After you've shared the strategy brief and the brand idea with them, explain how important their input is to the

> Here it's vital to have people from different departments and business lines to contribute to the process. This is the only way you will get widespread buy-in and support for actualizing your brand.

Institution X Brainstorm Map

"INSTITUTION X"
Brand • Purpose
FINANCIAL HEALTH for ALL

Internal:
- volunteer for Jr. Achievement
- robust 401K match
- coupon club
- investment club
- tuition reimbursement
- continuing ed
- banker cross training
- field trips to The Fed
- volunteer credit counselors
- mentors for employees
- book club
- volunteering at tax prep time
- unique sabbatical opps for longtime employees
- product innovation teams

External:
- kids' savings olympics
- webinars for business customers
- multiple online interest & payment calculators
- sponsor Jr. Achievement
- social media tips: savings & investing
- vault tours for kids
- online credit card analysis tools
- books by $$ experts to customers
- in-school branches
- $$ literacy classes for customer segments
- seminars for retail customers
- PSA-style ads promote savings & responsibility

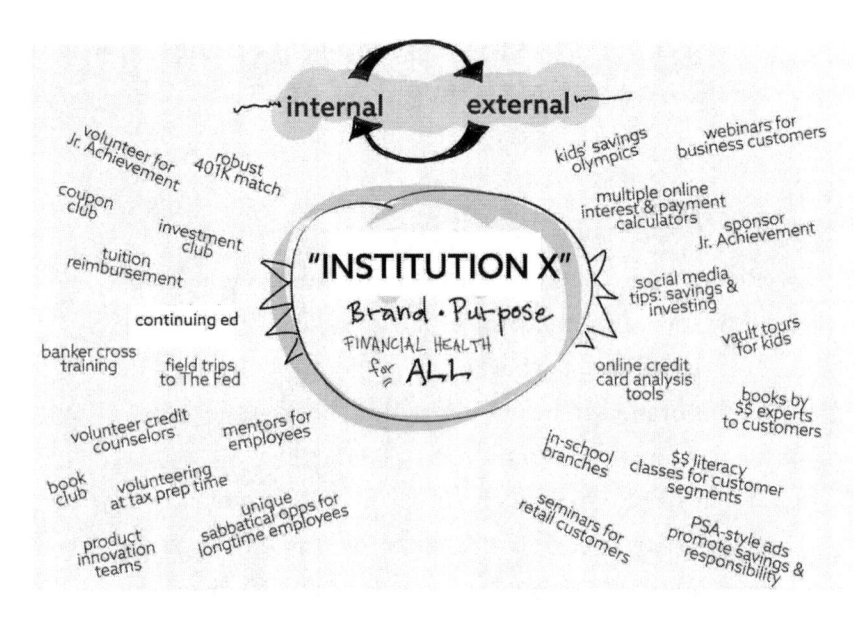

process. Share the brainstorm ground rules (from pages 103-105), then ask them to walk around the room and contribute ideas on each of the topics.

If your group is large, it will be helpful to have multiple papers with the same title next to each other to avoid bottlenecks.

Following are the main areas we recommend covering. There may be additional areas you want to address, depending on your institution and its purpose.

You may not have answers for every one of these bullet points. That's OK. They're

> No one needs to "stay in their lane." Everyone can—and should—contribute ideas around each business activity, no matter their role in the bank.

here to help you cover all the bases as you think about your Do Something brand.

Additionally, once you have the actions in place, they help you better evaluate opportunities that arise in the future. Do they sound fun, or do they actually help deliver on your brand promise?

For Employees:
- employee recognitions
- benefits
- culture
- personal and professional development (what it is and how it's administered)
- internal leadership programs
- mentorships and/or sponsorships
- financial education
- employee affinity groups

- take our kids/pets/parents to work days
- employee surveys
- advisory boards

For Employee Training to Work with Customers
- how to listen and counsel
- soft skills
- how the training will be delivered
- how often training is repeated or updated
- mode of conduct such as handshakes, hospitality, and addressing by first name or Mr./Ms./Mrs./Mx.

When Hiring
- position announcements
- social media posts
- "about us" copy on employment sites
- interviewing process
- onboarding experience

For Customer Communications
- email
- texts
- in-app messages
- mailings
- statement communications

For Customer Experience
- on-hold messaging, music, voice mail protocols

- branch locations, amenities, and functions
- drive-up
- website
- ATM
- banking app
- financial education
- advisory boards

For Sponsorships
- criteria for selection
- what the bank should expect in return

For Donations
- criteria for giving

For Branded Swag
- types of items
- item quality/cost
- guidelines for giving away to employees, customers, and prospects

For Volunteer Activities
- criteria for volunteering
- criteria for civic or nonprofit board service

For Advertising Media and Social Media Choices
- choices on where or where not to appear
- noting who can post, share, and comment on socials

For PR
- announcements about employee achievements
- announcements about bank milestones or anniversaries
- advocacy and/or education about a cause
- media relations
- influencer relations

For Special Events
- customer appreciation events
- partnerships with chamber of commerce and associations
- ribbon cuttings
- open house events

For Awards to Seek Out
- employer awards
- "best of" awards
- external awards for the bank
- external awards nominations for employees
- community leadership programs for employees

Find the gaps

Often, the internal side—the employee side—needs more attention.

- Once you've identified the holes, brainstorm with your team to develop more ideas worth exploring further.
- Find out where you need to do a better job communicating throughout the organization.

- Develop ways to let employees grow personally and professionally while they build your brand.
- Budget both time and money to adequately engage all audiences.
- Be sure to include people from all departments and at different levels. Avoid the pitfalls and silos that develop if you leave out your back-office teams. Every person in the bank plays a vital role in delivering on your brand promise—whether they face customers or not.

STEP 8. ANALYZE AND FINALIZE

If you dared to be stupid, it's most likely that you've got zillions of ideas. And we know it's impossible to implement them all. It will take discipline and nonjudgmental discussion to pare the ideas down to what's achievable.

It will be helpful to divide your group into subgroups: hiring, donations, marketing, customer experience, etc. and assign them to evaluate all the ideas in a particular category in a mini break-out session. At the appointed time, they can report their observations and recommendations to the larger group for feedback.

This does two things: 1) it helps streamline the process and 2) assures more buy-in since multiple people are able to discuss and influence the choices about what actions to implement.

As you come back together, ask each subgroup to walk the listeners through each of the big sheets of paper and make their remarks. Be sure to measure every idea back to your brand promise and your purpose to be sure they're a fit and they:

- Bring value to your audience personas.
- Differentiate your institution from others.
- Support the bank in making money.
- Naturally fit into your marketing plan.
- Don't present a reputational, operational, or legal risk.
- Are SMART: specific, measurable, attainable, relevant, and timely.

Also assess
- available resources
- ROI for each additional item
- budget
- time to implement
- time to generate results
- how it serves the goals

Break into phases: 6 months, 1 year, 2 years, 3 years

No one has enough time, money, or person-power to implement everything at once. As a leader, it's your job to work with your team to break these actions into those attainable and timely steps.

Determine what are the most vital things to do, and in what order.

> Employees should always hear about campaigns and changes before customers and the public see them.

If it's the former, you can start weaving these activities into marketing without a huge amount of fanfare. If, however, it's a relaunch or a rebrand, then you'll also need to orchestrate pre-launch and "TA DA!" strategies and tactics to unveil the new brand.

Assign Responsibilities

Now that you have tangible actions established, the work does not fall back on Marketing to get everything done. These actions need champions and doers. Marketing can't do it all. HR can't do it all. It will take leaders all across the organization to implement, sustain, measure, and grow. Who will own these items and ensure their success?

For a smaller initiative, it may only require one person to implement. For more complicated initiatives, it may take a sizable team. Marketing's role is really not changed from today's responsibilities:

> **Warning:** If there's an idea that everyone loves, but no one will champion, then it probably isn't a fit.

- Maintain the leadership perspective.
- Manage the big brand strategy.
- Be the glue that holds this brand puzzle together.
- Help recruit more colleagues to help.
- Monitor, gather measurements, and report out and up.

Don't confuse these responsibilities with the need to do everything. And just as deadly, the temptation to micro-manage everything. No one will stay on your team for long if you're breathing down their necks to watch every move.

Accountability: the Key to Staying on Track

Regular team meetings will be vital as you work to institute new ways of working and communicating. You may need to meet weekly or bi-weekly at first. As you get everything in sync and humming along, you can cut back on the number of meetings.

Always supplement these meetings with an internal shared digital document that allows people to update the status of their progress toward specific actions, goals, and the measurements that should follow. You can use the same document you developed in the planning stages as a starting point and add more fields for notes as needed.

Refer to it regularly to be sure deadlines and budgets are met. Note whether there seem to be any logjams with approvals or production starting to form. If you see that happening, be proactive. Assume the role of the diplomat who can intervene and reinstate the flow of work.

Out of Sight Should Not Be Out of Mind

Sustaining these brand action efforts requires care and feeding. Ensuring that you're staying on track involves more than just meetings. Observation and continuous stewardship will help you find out where internal communications should be strengthened, where additional training is needed, and where any processes may need to be refined.

Some ways to find out what's happening—especially if you have multiple branches in different markets:

Secret shopping: You can hire an agency that specializes in this service, or do some legwork yourself. Either way, establish the activities and brand engagements you want to measure and develop a standardized score sheet for consistency. "Shop" your branch, in person, online, social, and call center experiences at regular intervals.

Branch road shows: You and your team members can also hit the road and visit branches in person. During these visits, you can:

- Sit in the lobby to observe the surroundings and the personal interactions (employee-employee and employee-customer).

- Interview branch managers and personnel at different levels to gauge their understanding and get input.
- Ask for feedback and ideas on how to continue to improve brand activation.
- Conduct short, random customer surveys via text, phone, in online banking, or in-app messaging.

Chapter 11

PITFALLS TO WATCH OUT FOR

Just because you have a sparkly new brand doesn't mean you're immune to attack. Competition is fierce and aggressive. Players from new industries are seeking to lure customers' money away from FDIC- and NCUA-insured institutions. Pitfalls are all around.

While you strategize how to fend off the marauding outsiders, be sure you're not accidentally making your brand more vulnerable because of your own unintentional self-sabotaging actions.

HERE ARE 3 COMMON MISTAKES THAT WE SEE ON A REGULAR BASIS— AND HOW TO COMBAT THEM

1. Brand Fatigue

A lack of consistency in brand and sales promotions seems to run rampant with some institutions… those with

> A real-life example: A rogue branch decided to order bank logo attire with cute fonts and colors to match the local football team's colors.

brands that haven't been updated in ages, but also newly minted ones. It's as though the internal marketing people have grown weary of the same Pantone blue and gold and Century Gothic serif font. Or rogue teammates in Sales or HR want things to look jazzier and take it upon themselves to design some new collateral. Someone starts mixing things up.

We call it brand fatigue.

Suddenly, different product campaigns appear with varying color palettes, fonts, photography styles—or worse: alternating illustrations, bugs and photos from one campaign to the next.

You may be tired of seeing the same colors, fonts, and styles, but your audiences are not. You see these elements for more than 40 hours each week. Your audiences see them far less often. Don't assume your brand look has run its course simply because you're tired of it. Audiences need that repetition and reinforcement of your brand and what it offers. Don't distract and confuse them.

Famous brands like Nike have been faithful to their slogans and logos for decades. Their audiences are faithful too.

Quick self-test: Can you cover up the logo in an ad and immediately identify which institution is advertising? If not, there's a serious problem. It means money put toward developing the ad and paying for the media is tragically wasted.

2. Giving Up Too Soon

When developing new creative campaigns in-house or with their agency partners, some institutions make the mistake of falling in love with their first idea. They give up on pushing ideas further and settle for sameness.

Groupthink finds a home. Lack of originality runs rampant. Superheroes, smiling babies, blue skies, and other stock photo clichés are nearly ubiquitous in advertising from one bank to the next. While some of these concepts may be fun, they've been done to death.

If you look like and talk like everyone else, no one will know who you are. With far too many institutions that have the same or similar names, it's even more dangerous. When people Google "American Bank," they will get pages of results. If they haven't modified that search to be location-specific, they may click on a different bank than they want; if that bank's website looks like a bunch of others, it's a disservice to customers and the brand.

Therefore, be sure you're pushing past those first team brainstorm ideas. Dig deeper to uncover the gold nuggets that really set you apart.

You have to be different from the others and just like yourself.

3. Forgetting to Fly the Flag

Many times, banks launch product and sales promotions that are completely disconnected from their brand. Offerings that have no connection with their "why" and their purpose camouflage the brand and reinforce a commodity positioning.

The long version of your story is the language you use, the stories you tell, the songs you sing, and the camaraderie you share with colleagues and customers. These elements should all work together.

But your logo and slogan are like your country's flag: a shorthand symbol for your brand's meaning. The flag stirs hearts and minds. It gives focus and rallies the people. If you forget to raise it—or leave it in the dark—the people will lose their way.

Every single time you communicate, remember what you are here to do. Remind people how you are delivering it to customers and to each other. Why should people give their allegiance to your brand?

Make sure the signal is loud and clear.

There is no substitute for victory

You've made significant investments in your brand. Build and fiercely protect its equity from the inside out. Whether it's an ad campaign, an employee recruitment effort, social media or volunteer mission, it must surround and support your brand.

When it does, your strength will be incredibly difficult to overcome.

Afterword

LET'S GO!

Your brand evolution is an important one. And while it won't yield immediate results, it is probably the most important thing you can do as a marketer.

There is no doubt that short-term sales promotions like HELOC and checking acquisition campaigns are vital to producing short-term business results the bank needs to make money. So you have to make those the best they can be.

Savvy marketers have to juggle. They keep their eyes on the ball and look ahead at the same time.

A strong DO SOMETHING brand—once in play—will provide so much more lift for every sales promotion you undertake, you'll wonder why you didn't DO SOMETHING sooner.

You've got this.